SAS Statistics Data Analysis Interview Questions:

SAS Data Analysis Certification Review

Compiled By: Terry Sanchez-Clark

SAS Statistics Data Analysis Interview Questions: SAS Data Analysis Certification Review

ISBN: 978-1-60332-009-2

Edited By: Jamie Fisher

Printed in the United States of America

Please visit our website at www.itcookbook.com

Table of Contents

Introduction...7
Question 01: Installing SAS 9.1 on Windows XP 19
Question 02: Installing SAS for Windows Version 9x 20
Question 03: Creating Aliases for Variable Names in SAS......21
Question 04: Failure to start-up after using SAS 23
Question 05: Performing a Hierarchical Regression 25
Question 06: Presence of Spyware while installing 28
Question 07: SAS Java Cmponents.....................................30
Question 08: Installing SAS System Viewer 32
Question 09: Sample Code..33
Question 10: "OLE Object" error messages 34
Question 11: Import Wizard in SAS 35
Question 12: Installing SAS Windows 8.2 36
Question 13: SAS for Windows 8.2....................................38
Question 14: SAS Data Quality-Cleanse Software 39
Question 15: SAS Data Sets to open automatically 40
Question 16: Using SAS®9 for Windows 41
Question 17: Storing Output Delivery System (Version 7 and higher)..42
Question 18: Getting the Current Output 43
Question 19: Import Wizard..44
Question 20: Removing Header Text from SAS Output Pages
....45
Question 21: Setting SAS System.......................................47
Question 22: "Host Internal Error: 11" problem on SAS Icon48
Question 23: Running DOS command...............................49
Question 24: Page Breaks...50
Question 25: Installation of Software on Windows.................52
Question 26: SAS Data Set 55
Question 27: Double Space Output 56
Question 28: Proc Mixed..57
Question 29: Renaming Entry Point in SAS 9.......................58
Question 30: Threaded Kernel...59
Question 31: Transport Files..60
Question 32: Displaying a list of Metadata Server................61
Question 33: Disabling Macro Prompt in Excel....................62
Question 34: Reading HTML table..64
Question 35: Replacing the opening page break....................68
Question 36: Uninstall SAS System 70
Question 37: Hiding code 71
Question 38: Creating a Variable indicating a Percentile.......72
Question 39: Removing duplicates in Data Set 73

Question 40: Suppressing the automatic printing in output .74
Question 41: Suppressing Page Ejects 75
Question 42: Release 6.07...76
Question 43: Putting the value of BY Variable 77
Question 44: Converting SAS Dataset 78
Question 45: Suppress warnings in SAS Log 81
Question 46: Checking co linearity in Logistic Regression....82
Question 47: Fixing Procedures that are formatted differently
....83
Question 48: SAS Site Number 85
Question 49: SAS/INTRNET-Frequently asked questions and
Hints..86
Question 50: Accessing Auto call Macro library.....................88
Question 51: Accessing Sample Library Programs.................90
Question 52: Experimental Software.......................................93
Question 53: Creating an Output Data Set 94
Question 54: Services from Statistical Technical Support......96
Question 55: Sensitivity Analysis..97
Question 56: Procedures for Analysis Survey Data Base 98
Question 57: Alternative Methods for Neural Networks........99
Question 58: Reading SAS Date values (and other numeric
data) from a string variable...100
Question 59: "n equations" 101
Question 60: Creating Design Matrix in a Data Set..............103
Question 61: Character-to-Numeric Conversions and
Numeric-to-Character Conversions..106
Question 62: Launching SAS under UNIX.............................109
Question 63: Exporting SAS Dataset 112
Question 64: SAS/Access to Oracle..113
Question 65: SAS/Access Interface to PC File Formats.........114
Question 66: Using SAS Data Sets with *.sd7 extensions in
Version 9...115
Question 67: Determining Schema 116
Question 68: Setting Program Editor Colors in SAS under
UNIX..117
Question 69: Finding your IP address when Using SAS for
UNIX under Micro-X or Mac-X...118
Question 70: Launching SAS for UNIX in an X-Win session in
the ITS Public User Areas..119
Question 71: Sending an SAS Dataset through e-mail...........121
Question 72: Size of an SAS Data Set....................................123
Question 73: Writing SAS Data Set into Raw Data...............124
Question 74: Garbage Characters in SAS for Windows Output
files...126

Question 75: Truncation of SAS numeric values....................127
Question 76: Redirecting SAS Log and Output......................128
Question 77: Using SPSS Data (Portable File) in SAS..........129
Question 78: Using SAS Data (Transport File) in SPSS........136
Question 79: Converting Access, Excel, and dBase-type files into SAS Data Sets..139
Question 80: Dealing with Date Values from Excel or Access Databases...147
Question 81: Lost Variables (Columns) when Importing Data from Other Software...151
Question 82: Preserving Formatted Values When Moving SAS Data to Spreadsheet Software..152
Question 83: SAS Transport Files 157
Question 84: Converting Old SAS FSEDIT Screens and other SAS Catalogs to Version 8.x..161
Question 85: Using a Macintosh SAS Program File in SAS for Windows..162
Question 86: Using e-macs instead of the SAS Program Editor in Interactive SAS...163
Question 87: Using Compressed Data Stored on UNIX Disk or UniTree..164
Question 88: Using Data Files Larger than 2 GB.................166
Question 89: Floating Point Overflow Errors in PROC LOGISTIC..171
Question 90: SAS Add-ons needs other SAS Modules to run Windows and Macintosh...172
Question 91: Software that works with SAS 173
Question 92: Selecting Observations in a Merge..................174
Question 93: Reading in to SAS data files with special delimiters...177
Question 94: Writing out from SAS data files with special delimiters...181
Question 95: SAS across Different Systems...........................184
Question 96: Recoding Variables with a Data Array.............190
Question 97: Changing the Internal Order of Variables in an SAS Data Set..193
Question 98: Selecting a given word from a Variable Value.194
Question 99: Converting SAS Files for use in Version 9.1 -- PROC MIGRATE...195
Question 100: Setting FTP download mode in SAS..............198
Question 101: Reading SAS Data Sets in SAS Release 7........199
Question 102: Special considerations in Release 7 and higher 201
Question 103: Database Permissions to run Scheduler........203

Question 104: Array Statements..204
Question 105: Estimating the distribution of sample data...205
Question 106: Using Version 7 206
Question 107: Determining the polygon selected point 208
Question 108: Making Windows stay in foreground............211
Question 109: Adding label to the new point........................212
Question 110: Scheduler Parameters....................................213
Question 111: Formats that export files can use...................214
Question 112: Installing SAS for Windows...........................215
Question 113: Creating Version 6.12 SAS Data Set...............216
Question 114: SAS under UNIX Release 7............................218
Question 115: Changing name of a layer on SAS/GIS map . .219
Question 116: Equation for a nonparametric regression model
....220
Question 117: Rearranging Data 222
Question 118: Reading the rest of Variables 227
Question 119: Repetitive DATA steps 230
Question 120: Periods as Missing Values in Character Data 232
Question 121: Transposing Row Data into Columns, and
Columns into Rows...233
Question 122: Collapsing Multiple Records 238
Question 123: Rectangular varying number of observations
....242
Question 124: Creating "Lag" variables 246
Question 125: Using Values Stored in an SAS Data Set as
Macro Variables in a Macro..247
Question 126: Using an SAS Data Set as a 'Lookup' File for
Merging...251
Question 127: Reading SAS Date values (and other numeric
data) from a string variable..254
Question 128: Paired T-Tests- SAS Uses PROC MEANS (!). 255
Question 129: Computing points along the curve of a
theoretical distribution 258
Acknowledgment..259
Index..260

Introduction

The SAS System, originally Statistical Analysis System, is an integrated system of software products provided by SAS Institute that enables the programmer to perform:

* Data entry, retrieval, management, and mining
* Report writing and graphics
* Statistical and mathematical analysis
* Business planning, forecasting, and decision support
* Operations research and project management
* Quality improvement
* Applications development
* Data warehousing (extract, transform, load)
* Platform independent and remote computing

In addition, the SAS System integrates with many SAS business solutions that enable large-scale software solutions for areas such as human resource management, financial management, business intelligence, customer relationship management and more.

Description of SAS

SAS 8 on an IBM Mainframe under 3270 emulation
SAS 8 on an IBM Mainframe under 3270 emulation

SAS is driven by SAS programs that define a sequence of operations to be performed on data stored as tables. Although non-programmer graphical user interfaces to SAS exist (such as the SAS Enterprise Guide), most of the time these GUIs are just a front-end to automate or facilitate generation of SAS programs. SAS components expose their functionalities via application programming interfaces, in the form of statements and procedures.

An SAS program is composed of three major parts.

1. The DATA step
2. Procedure steps (effectively, everything that is not enclosed in a DATA step)
3. Macro language

SAS Library Engines and Remote Library Services allow access to data stored in external data structures and on remote computer platforms.

The DATA step section of an SAS program, like other database-oriented fourth-generation programming languages such as SQL or Focus, assumes a default file structure; and automates the process of identifying files to the operating system, opening the input file, reading the next record, opening the output file, writing the next record, and closing the files. This allows the user/programmer to concentrate on the details of working with the data within each record – in effect working almost entirely within an implicit program loop that runs for each record.

All other tasks are accomplished by procedures that operate on the data set (SAS' terminology for "table") as a whole. Typical tasks include printing or performing statistical analysis, and may just require the user/programmer to identify the data set. Procedures are not restricted to only one behavior and thus allow extensive customization, controlled by mini-languages defined within the procedures. SAS also has an extensive SQL procedure, allowing SQL programmers to use the system with little additional knowledge.

There are macro programming extensions, that allow for rationalization of repetitive sections of the program. Proper imperative and procedural programming constructs can be simulated by use of the "open code" macros or the SAS/IML component.

Macro code in an SAS program, if any, undergoes preprocessing. At runtime, DATA steps are compiled and procedures are interpreted and run in the sequence they appear in the SAS program. AN SAS program requires the SAS System to run.

Compared to general-purpose programming languages, this structure allows the user/programmer to be less familiar with the technical details of the data and how it is stored, and relatively more familiar with the information contained in the data. This blurs the line between user and programmer, appealing to individuals who fall more into the 'business' or 'research' area and less in the 'information technology' area, since SAS does not enforce (although SAS recommends) a structured, centralized approach to data and infrastructure management.

The SAS System runs on IBM mainframes, Unix machines, OpenVMS Alpha, and Microsoft Windows; and code is almost transparently moved between these environments. Older versions have supported PC-DOS, the Apple Macintosh, VMS, VM/CMS, Data General AOS and OS/2.

Early History of SAS

SAS was conceived by Anthony J. Barr in 1966.[1] As a North Carolina State University graduate student from 1962 to 1964, Barr had created an analysis of variance modeling language inspired by the notation of statistician Maurice Kendall, followed by a multiple regression program that generated machine code for performing algebraic transformations of the raw data. Drawing on those programs and his experience with structured data files[2], he created SAS, placing statistical procedures into a formatted file framework. From 1966 to 1968, Barr developed the fundamental structure and language of SAS.

In January 1968, Barr and James Goodnight collaborated, integrating new multiple regression and analysis of variance routines developed by Goodnight into Barr's framework.[3][4] Goodnight's routines made the handling of basic statistical analysis more robust, and his later implementation (in SAS 76) of the general linear model greatly increased the analytical power of the system. By 1971, the SAS system was gaining popularity within the academic community. And by 1972, industry was making use of SAS. One strength of the system was analyzing experiments with missing data, which was useful to the pharmaceutical and agricultural industries, among others.

In 1973, John P. Sall joined the project, making extensive programming contributions in econometrics, time series, and matrix algebra. Other participants in the early years included Caroll G. Perkins, Jolayne W. Service, and Jane T. Helwig. Perkins made programming contributions. Service and Helwig created the early documentation.[3]

In 1976, SAS Institute, Inc. was incorporated by Barr, Goodnight, Sall, and Helwig.

The SAS system consists of a number of components, which organizations separately license and install as required.

SAS Add-In for Microsoft Office

A component of the SAS Enterprise Business Intelligence Server, is designed to provide access to data, analysis, reporting and analytics for non-technical workers (such as business analysts, power users, domain experts and decision makers) via menus and toolbars integrated into Office applications.

Base SAS

The core of the SAS System is the so-called Base SAS Software, which is used to manage data. SAS procedures software analyzes and reports the data. The SQL procedure allows SQL programming in lieu of data step and procedure programming. Library Engines allow transparent access to common data structures such as Oracle, as well as pass-through of SQL to be executed by such data structures.

The Macro facility is a tool for extending and customizing SAS software programs and reducing overall program verbosity. The DATA step debugger is a programming tool that helps find logic problems in DATA step programs. The Output Delivery System (ODS) is an extendable system that delivers output in a variety of formats, such as SAS data sets, listing files, RTF, PDF, XML, or HTML.

The SAS windowing environment is an interactive, graphical user interface used to run and test SAS programs.

SAS Enterprise Business Intelligence Server: includes both a suite of business intelligence (BI) tools and a platform to provide uniform access to data. The goal of this product is to compete with Business Objects and Cognos' offerings.

Enterprise Computing Offer (ECO): not to be confused with Enterprise Guide or Enterprise Miner, ECO is a product bundle.

Enterprise Guide: is a Microsoft Windows client application that provides a guided mechanism to use SAS and publish dynamic results throughout an organization in an uniform way. It is marketed as the default interface to SAS for business analysts, statisticians, and programmers.

Enterprise Miner: it is a data-mining tool.

ETL: provides Extract, transform, load services.

SAS/ACCESS: provides the ability for SAS to transparently share data with non-native data sources.

SAS/ACCESS for PC Files: allows SAS to transparently share data with personal computer applications including MS Access and Microsoft Office Excel.

SAS/AF: Applications facility, a set of application development tools to create customized applications.

SAS/ASSIST: early point-and-click interface to the SAS system, has since been superseded by SAS Enterprise Guide.

SAS/C

SAS/CONNECT: provides ability for SAS sessions on different platforms to communicate with each other.

SAS/DMI: a programming interface between interactive SAS and ISPF/PDF applications. Obsolete since version 5.

SAS/EIS: a menu-driven system for developing, running, and maintaining an enterprise information systems.

SAS/ETS: provides Econometrics and Time Series Analysis.

SAS/FSP: allows interaction with data using integrated tools for data entry, computation, query, editing, validation, display, and retrieval.

SAS/GIS: an interactive desktop Geographic Information System for mapping applications.

SAS/GRAPH: although base SAS includes primitive graphing capabilities, SAS/GRAPH is needed for charting on graphical media.

SAS/IML: Matrix-handling SAS script extensions.

SAS/INSIGHT: is a dynamic tool for data mining. Allows examination of uni-variate distributions, visualization of multi-variate data, and model fitting using regression, analysis of variance, and the generalized linear model.

SAS/IntrNet: it extends SAS' data retrieval and analysis functionality to the Web with a suite of CGI and Java tools.

SAS/LAB: is superseded by SAS Enterprise Guide.

SAS/OR: Operations Research

SAS/PH: Clinical Defunct product

SAS/QC: quality control provides quality improvement tools.

SAS/SHARE: is a data server that allows multiple users to gain simultaneous access to SAS files

SAS/STAT: Statistical Analysis with a number of procedures, providing statistical information such as analysis of variance, regression, multi-variate analysis, and categorical data analysis.

SAS/TOOLKIT

SAS/Warehouse Administrator: Superseded in SAS 9 by SAS ETL Server.

SAS Web Report Studio: Part of the SAS Enterprise Business Intelligence Server, provides access to query and reporting capabilities on the Web. Aimed at non-technical users.

Example SAS code

SAS uses data steps and procedures to analyze and manipulate data. By default, a data step iterates through each observation in a data set (sort of like every row in a SQL table).

This data step creates a new data set BBB that includes those observations from data set AAA that had charges greater than 100.

```
data BBB;

set AAA;

if charge > 100;
```

```
run;
```

Procedures that can summarize data are available in SAS. The proc freq procedure shows a frequency distribution of a given variable in a data set.

```
proc freq data=BBB;

table charge;

run;
```

SAS features a macro language, which can be used to generate SAS code. For instance, the above example could be re-used in many pieces of code by rewriting it as a macro:

```
%macro freqtable(table, variable);

proc freq data = &table;

table &variable;

run;

%mend freqtable;

%freqtable(BBB, charge)
```

SAS has a useful feature where it can display the queried information. The proc print procedure is used for this:

```
proc print data=BBB;
run;
```

Version History

SAS 71

SAS 71 was the first limited release of the system. The first manual for SAS was printed at this time, approximately 60 pages long[5]. The DATA step was implemented. Regression and analysis of variance were the main uses of the program.

SAS 72

This more robust release was the first to achieve wide distribution. It included a substantial user's guide, 260 pages in length[6]. The MERGE statement was introduced in this release, adding the ability to perform a database JOIN on two data sets[7]. This release also introduced the comprehensive handling of missing data[8].

SAS 76

SAS 76 was a complete system level rewrite, featuring an open architecture for adding and extending procedures, and for extending the compiler[9]. The INPUT and INFILE statements were significantly enhanced to read virtually all data formats in use on the IBM mainframe[10]. Report generation was added through the PUT and FILE statements[11]. The capacity to analyze general linear models was added[12].

Version 79.3 - 82.4

1980 saw the addition of SAS/GRAPH, a graphing component; and SAS/ETS for econometric and time series analysis. In 1981 SAS/FSP followed, providing full-screen interactive data entry, editing, browsing, retrieval, and letter writing.

In 1983 full-screen spreadsheet capabilities were introduced (PROC FSCALC).

Version 4 series

In the early 1980s, SAS Institute released Version 4, the first version for non-IBM computers. It was written mostly in a subset of the PL/I language, to run on several minicomputer manufacturers' operating systems and hardware: Data General's AOS/VS, Digital Equipment's VAX/VMS, and Prime Computer's PRIMOS. The version was colloquially called "Portable SAS" because most of the code was portable, i.e., the same code would run under different operating systems.

Version 5 series

Version 5 was the release used through the late 1980s and lingered on in many institutions well into the 1990s. It was the last version written mainly in PL/I.

Version 6 series

Version 6 represented a major milestone for SAS. While it was superficially similar to the user, the major change was "under the hood", where the software was rewritten. From its FORTRAN origins, followed by PL/I and mainframe assembly language; in version 6 the SAS System was rewritten in C, to provide enhanced portability between operating systems, as well as access to an increasing pool of C programmers compared to the shrinking pool of PL/I programmers.

This was the first version to run on UNIX, MS-DOS and Windows platforms. The DOS versions were incomplete implementations of the Version 6 spec: some functions and formats were unavailable, as were SQL and related items such as indexing and WHERE subsetting. DOS memory limitations restricted the size of some user-defined items.

In 1984 a project management component was added (SAS/OR?).

In 1985 SAS/AF software, econometrics and time series analysis (SAS/DMI) component, and interactive matrix programming (SAS/IML) software was introduced. MS-DOS SAS (version 6.02) was introduced, along with a link to mainframe SAS.

In 1986 Statistical quality improvement component is added (SAS/QC software); SAS/IML and SAS/STAT software is released for personal computers.

1987 saw concurrent update access provided for SAS data sets with SAS/SHARE software. Database interfaces are introduced for DB2 and SQL-DS.

In 1988 Multi Vendor Architecture (MVA) concept is introduced; SAS/ACCESS software is released. Support for UNIX-based hardware announced. SAS/ASSIST software for building user-friendly front-end menus is introduced. New SAS/CPE software establishes SAS as innovator in computer performance evaluation. Version 6.03 for MS-DOS is released.

6.06 for MVS, CMS, and OpenVMS is announced in 1990. The same year, the last MS-DOS version (6.04) is released.

Data visualization capabilities added in 1991 with SAS/INSIGHT software.

In 1992 SAS/CALC, SAS/TOOLKIT, SAS/PH-Clinical, and SAS/LAB software is released.

In 1993 software for building customized executive information systems (EIS) is introduced. Release 6.08 for MVS, CMS, VMS, VSE, OS/2, and Windows is announced.

1994 saw the addition of ODBC support, plus SAS/SPECTRAVIEW and SAS/SHARE*NET components.

6.09 saw the addition of a data step debugger.

6.09E for MVS.

6.10 in 1995 was a Microsoft Windows release and the first release for the Apple Macintosh. Version 6 was the first, and last series to run on the Macintosh.

Also in 1995, 6.11 (code named Orlando) was released for Windows 95, Windows NT, and UNIX.

6.12 were Unix and Microsoft Windows releases (and more?)

(Some of the following milestones in this sub-section may belong under version 7 or 8.)

In 1996 SAS announces Web enablement of SAS software. Scalable performance data server is introduced.

In 1997 SAS/Warehouse Administrator and SAS/InterNet software goes into production.

1998 sees SAS introduce a customer relationship management (CRM) solution, and an ERP access interface — SAS/ACCESS interface for SAP R/3. SAS is also the first to release OLE-DB for

OLAP and releases HOLAP solution. Balanced scorecard, SAS/Enterprise Reporter, and HR Vision are released. First release of SAS Enterprise Miner.

1999 sees the releases of HR Vision software, the first end-to-end decision-support system for human resources reporting and analysis; and Risk Dimensions software, an end-to-end risk-management solution. MS-DOS versions are abandoned because of Y2K issues and lack of continued demand.

In 2000 SAS shipped Enterprise Guide and ported its software to Linux.

Version 7 series

The Output Delivery System debuted in version 7; as did long variable names (from 8 to 32 characters); storage of long character strings in variables (from 200 to 32,767); and a much improved built-in text editor, the Enhanced Editor.

Version 7 saw the synchronization of features between the various platforms for a particular version number (which previously hadn't been the case).

Version 7 was a precursor to version 8. It was believed SAS Institute released a snapshot from their development on version 8 to meet a deadline promise. SAS Institute recommended that sites wait until version 8 before deploying the new software.

Version 8 series

Released about 1999; 8.0, 8.1, 8.2 were Unix, Microsoft Windows, and z/OS releases. Key features: long variable names, Output Delivery System (ODS).

Version 9 series

In version 9, SAS Institute added the SAS Management Console, parallel processing, JavaObj, ODS OO (experimental as opposed to alpha), and National Language Support.

Again the SAS Institute recommended sites delay deployment until 9.1.

SAS Version 9 is running on Windows (32 & 64 bit), Unix (64 bit), Linux, and z/OS.

SAS 9.1 was released in 2003.

SAS 9.1.2 was released in 2004.

SAS 9.1.3 was released in 2005.

SAS 9.1.3 Service Pack 4 is the latest release (April 2006).

SAS 9.2 is the next release [1] and was demonstrated at the SUGI31 Conference in March 2006[2]. Possible release between March 2007 and June 2007.

Question 01: Installing SAS 9.1 on Windows XP

I'm installing SAS 9.1.x on Windows XP Home Edition, and the verification of the "minimum system requirements" failed. It prevents me from installing SAS itself.

Is it still possible to install SAS under these circumstances?

A: SAS Institute supports the installation of SAS Version 9.1.x on Windows XP Professional, but not Windows XP Home Edition. The specific problem is that the minimum system requirements that SAS checks and updates before the main install procedure cannot be updated in the way SAS wants them to be updated.

It may be possible to bypass the minimum system requirements and install SAS but doing this is not supported by SAS Institute. ITS will still try to help with any problems you might have, but if SAS Institute needs to be called, they will remind us that installing on Windows XP Home is not supported.

Try a workaround,

Click Start > Run and, in the command field, type:

E:\SAS\setup.exe nomsupdate

Note: The example uses "E:\" as the drive where the SAS Setup CD is loaded. If your CD drive is assigned a different letter, you would use that letter instead of "E:\".

Question 02: Installing SAS for Windows Version 9x

How can I install SAS for Windows Version 9.x on the Windows ME platform?

A: The last version of SAS for Windows that was supported under Windows ME was Version 8.2 SAS Institute says that Windows ME doesn't use memory efficiently enough to allow Version 9.x to run.

You have two options in this situation:

1. ITS can distribute Version 8.2, and if you change operating systems during the time you are licensed (i.e., before your expiration date) you can get the most current version of SAS for Windows without charge from ITS.

2. You can upgrade your Windows operating system to XP.

Question 03: Creating Aliases for Variable Names in SAS

I have a Dataset with several variables. How can I create symbolic names for subsets of variables to avoid retyping large blocks of names in analysis?

The PROC's I use include MEANS, SYSLIN and REG. The variable names are descriptive and do not have the same root (as in VAR1, VAR2, etc).

A: Here's how you can create it.

1. Use the %LET statement at the beginning of your program to create names to stand for the variable groupings, and then call these names in to your programs as needed.

    Here is an example:

    ```
    %LET PERSONS = JERRY ANDREW MARY JOHN FRED;

    %LET PLACES  = MODESTO FRESNO COALINGA MARIPOSA
    ALTURAS;

    %LET THINGS  = FORK KNIFE SPOON PLATE CUP SAUCER
    DISH;

    %LET ALL     = &PERSONS &PLACES &THINGS ;

    OPTIONS SYMBOLGEN MPRINT;  /* To see the
    'resolved' values in the Log */
    ```

2. Set OPTIONS MPRINT and SYMBOLGEN in your options statement so you can see what SAS do to execute this code. This is not necessary but handy for debugging.

    Now, you can refer to all variables in the three strings like this:

    ```
    OPTIONS DQUOTE;

    TITLE "Analysis using &PLACES";
    ```

```
PROC REG;

MODEL INCOME = &PLACES;

RUN;

TITLE "Means of &THINGS";

PROC MEANS DATA=MYDATA(keep=&THINGS);

RUN;
```

You can refer to two or three groups at the same time:

```
PROC REG;

MODEL INCOME = &PLACES &THINGS;

RUN;

PROC MEANS;

VAR &ALL;

PROC FREQ;

TABLES &PERSONS &PLACES;
```

Question 04: Failure to start-up after using SAS

After using SAS for Windows, it either fails completely to start up or get a version of the following message:

ERROR: Read Access Violation In Task [sasxkern]
Exception occurred at [676B6E1A]
Task Traceback

or

Note: Unable to open sasuser.profile. Instead work.profile is opened.

Note: All profile changes will be lost at the end of the session.

When installing or invoking Version 7 or higher, SAS may be unable to open existing Profiles and/or Registry files. The problem is that one or more of the files, Profile.sas7bcat, Profile2.sas7bcat or Registry.sas7bitm, have become corrupted. This doesn't happen often, and no one specific cause is known when it does happen.

A: Rename the three files to any name different from the original, such as profile.001, profile2.001, and registry.001 then restart the SAS System. This will create new profiles.

The profiles are stored in your SASUSER library. By default, this library is placed in

C:\Documents and Settings\\My Documents\My SAS Files\9.1

Though some users ask SAS to place the SASUSER library in other locations. If the Profile and Registry files are not in the default location, you can usually find out where they are by looking in your SASv9.CFG file and/or the Properties tab of your SAS startup icon. If SAS is starting, and you're just trying to fix messages you see in the Log, you can determine the location of the SASUSER library by typing libname at the command line (the field at the upper left of your SAS window with the check-mark symbol to the left of it).

PROFILE files are used for storing configuration information for the SAS Display Manager (the SAS Windows), Function Key settings, and other features. Any permanent changes you make to the appearance of the Display Manager, such as shape, position, color, etc., or changes in the way the Function Keys are programmed, and so forth, are stored in the PROFILE file(s). If you do customize your SAS Session in these ways, it is always a good idea to make backup copies of the PROFILE file(s) so that in the unlikely event that the file(s) get corrupted, you can replace them with backup copies, and you won't have to re-set all your customized features.

To make backups, simply go into your SASUSER directory, right-click on each file icon, and choose "Copy", then right-click again and choose "Paste". This will create Copy files. You might want to rename them, then, to something like profile.backup and profile2.backup for future reference. If the Profiles get corrupted, you would then reverse the process: delete or rename profile.sas7bcat and profile2.sas7bcat, then right-click on the icons for profile.backup and profile2.backup then "Copy" then "Paste" and re-name the copied files to the original profile names of profile.sas7bcat and profile2.sas7bcat.

Question 05: Performing a Hierarchical Regression

How can I perform a Hierarchical Regression using SAS?

A: SAS can do a Hierarchical Regression using either PROC REG with a TEST statement, or with the new TESTS and SEQTESTS options. The TESTS and SEQTESTS options are considered experimental in Version 8, and are not yet documented.

EXAMPLES:

For a Hierarchical Regression, perhaps the clearest approach is to use PROC REG and its TEST statement. Consider the following code.

```
PROC REG;

MODEL y = x2 x3;

TEST x3=0, x2=0;

MODEL y = x1 x2 x3 x4;

TEST x1=0, x4=0;

RUN;
```

The first TEST statement produces a test of the null hypothesis that the predictor vectors x2 and x3 are both equal to zero. This is equivalent to the hypothesis that these two variables add no predictive ability to the model (in this case, to the null model consisting only of the grand mean).

The second TEST statement tests whether the variables x1 and x4 add any predictive ability to the model containing x2 and x3 (and the grand mean). Each TEST statement must be interpreted relative to the MODEL statement preceding it.

Another approach is to consider is described in the following information. Beginning with Version 8 of the SAS System, the

TESTS and SEQTESTS options have been added to the SCORR1 and SCORR2 options on the MODEL statement to provide this information. However, these options were not added in time to be documented. The documentation follows:

The TESTS and SEQTESTS options have been added to the SCORR1 and SCORR2 options to provide tests as variables are sequentially added to a model in PROC REG. The syntax is as follows:

```
MODEL Y=X1-X5/SCORR1(TESTS);
```

Or

```
MODEL Y=X1-X5/SCORR1(SEQTESTS);
```

And similarly for SCORR2.

These options produce F-tests which are calculated as the sum of squares for the variable in question divided by the mean square error for the full model. If TESTS is specified, the MSE for the complete model (the MSE from the ANOVA table) is used as the denominator. If SEQTESTS is specified, the full model (and MSE associated with it) changes as variables are added sequentially to the regression model.

For example, the following is a table of parameter estimates for a regression of a dependent variable on five independent variables, X1-X5. The MODEL statement was: MODEL Y=X1-X5/SCORR1(SEQTESTS);

```
                  Parameter Estimates

               Parameter    Standard
Variable   DF   Estimate     Error    t Value   Pr > |t|

Intercept  1    1.21230     0.18273     6.63     <.0001
X1         1   -0.15058     0.14669    -1.03     0.3059
X2         1   -0.05647     0.15469    -0.37     0.7155
X3         1    0.14848     0.14674     1.01     0.3129
X4         1    2.95669     0.13822    21.39     <.0001
X5         1    4.65109     0.15843    29.36     <.0001
```

Parameter Estimates

Variable	DF	Squared Semi-partial Corr Type I	Cumulative R-Square	-Sequential F Value	TypeI- Pr > F
Intercept	1	.	0	.	.
X1	1	0.00083606	0.00083606	0.17	0.6844
X2	1	0.00957	0.01041	1.91	0.1690
X3	1	0.00123	0.01163	0.24	0.6224
X4	1	0.33511	0.34675	100.03	<.0001
X5	1	0.53322	0.87997	861.81	<.0001

The column titled Squared Semi-partial Corr Type I contains the normal output from the SCORR1 option. These are the partial R-Squares. The next column over contains the Cumulative R-Square. This is the R-Square from the previous model plus the partial R-Square for the current variable. Next is the sequential F-test, calculated as mentioned above, and its associated p-value.

Note:

1. These options are considered experimental in Version 8 and are not documented.

2. These options do not work with the model selection methods, the RIDGE or PCOMIT options or with the GROUPNAMES= option.

Question 06: Presence of Spyware while installing

When installing SAS 9.1x, the process hangs during the near end of the process. And the only solution seems to be a cold reboot power down and restart.

What seems to be the problem?

A: The cause of your problem has something to do with the presence of Spyware or Adware on your computer. The SAS installation may also require temporarily turning off the software that protects you against further Spyware or Adware intrusions just as it suggests that you (temporarily) close virus protection software.

You can find detection and removal software for Adware and/or Spyware on the internet.

You might also consider using a Web browser other than Internet Explorer, the security "holes" in Internet Explorer may be admitting some Spyware and/or Adware evildoers. Other choices include Netscape and Mozilla.

SAS Institute lists a number of other possible causes for installation problems, including (but not only) the following:

1. Virus protection software running in the background (this should be disabled before attempting to install SAS).

2. You need to be logged in as Administrator when installing SAS.

3. Stray SAS processes (check the Windows Task Manager for multiple instances of sas.exe running)

4. Bad printer drivers (the problem here may not be apparent during the install, but bad printer drivers can result in the already- installed SAS software not being able to start up; solution is to delete and reinstall printer drivers, ideally deleting them before the SAS install, and reinstalling them

after, though simply deleting/reinstalling the printer drivers
might be enough)

Another suggestion they have is to boot in Safe Mode (this
technique differs, depending on your operating system. Make
sure to uninstall and/or remove any remnants of SAS 9.1 that
might have been installed, even partially.

Another suggestion (after cleaning up any previous partial install
remnants, of course) is the following:

1. Click Start/Run to get a run dialog up and put the SAS/Setup
    cd in your CD-ROM drive.

2. Click Browse and go to the CD-ROM location; migrate down
    into the SAS folder; double click on the setup.exe that is in
    the SAS folder; this will put a string in the Run dialog Open
    line.

3. Place your mouse cursor at the end of the line and add a
    space.

4. Type in the following two options:

    noreboot nomsupdate

    then click "OK". This will start the install directly.

Question 07: SAS Java Cmponents

When running ODS Graphics after installing SAS 9.1 or higher (or other features), I see a message such as:

"Unable to load the Java Virtual Machine"

Or some other message that indicates one of the system requirements that the SAS Installer is supposed to check and install has been corrupted or is otherwise unavailable.

A: The SAS Java component and certain other software are installed by the SAS System Requirements Wizard when it inspects the system and determines that they need to be installed. It is possible for these system components to be uninstalled or otherwise unavailable to the system, but still appear to be installed and running.

In this case, it may be necessary to install them "manually", i.e., without using the normal SAS Setup procedure.

To install the SAS Java Runtime Environment software:

1. Click Start > Control Panel > Add/Remove Programs and highlight, then remove, the "Java Runtime Components (SAS Version)"

2. Insert and open (explore) the SAS Setup CD and click srw > bundles > sasjre (srw stands for System Requirement Wizard and sasjre stands for SAS Java Runtime Environment)

3. Click (run) the jresetup.exe file and follow all instructions.

To install the other system requirements:

1. Insert and open (explore) the SAS Setup CD and click srw > redist.

2. Click (run) the folder icon for the component you need to install; some folders will have an *.exe to run at the first level inside the folder; other folders will have various folders with

two-letter names -- these are the various languages available (for English, click the folder labeled en) -- and the *.exe will be inside these folders.

3. Click (run) the *.exe in the folder you've chosen. If that component is already installed, you will see a message to that effect. Otherwise, SAS will install it for you.

Question 08: Installing SAS System Viewer

How can I install SAS System Viewer without using my CDs?

A: For Version 9.1 and higher, the USC distribution of SAS for Windows includes the SAS System Viewer on Software Disk 2.

For all versions, it is available at the SAS Web site for free download.

Note that this SAS Institute Web page refers to the "Client-Side Components Volume 1" CD. However, for the ITS/USC distribution version, the System Viewer is contained on the Software Disk 2 CD.

To install from the USC CD, open the "systemviewer" folder and click on the SASView91.exe file to start the install process.

Though the above document references SAS 9.1 in its instructions, the download instructions are applicable no matter what recent Version of SAS for Windows you are running.

Note also that you will need to register and login at the SAS Web site in order to download the SAS System Viewer. This is noted in the document referenced above.

Question 09: Sample Code

This contains short examples of SAS code that is either new to the SAS System, or useful-but-obscure.

The SELECT Loop

Multiple IF statements in a DATA Step can be replaced with the more efficient SELECT Loop.
If you will normally write:

```
if region='South' then quarter=4;

else if region='North' then quarter=3;

else if region='East' then quarter=2;

else quarter=1;
```

A: You can accomplish the same thing with the SELECT Loop in a DATA Step:

```
select(region);

when('South') quarter=4;

when('North') quarter=3;

when('East') quarter=2;

1 otherwise quarter=1;

end;
```

Question 10: "OLE Object" error messages

After installing SAS for Windows (Version 8 or 9), I start up SAS and there is no Program Editor and there are "OLE object" error messages or a message in the Log:

ERROR: SAS Syntax Editor Control is not installed

A: Once in a while, some combination of the Operating System, the SAS Modules and other elements causes a minor part of SAS Version 8 not to get installed. This can be fixed easily if you re-insert the SAS Shared Components CD (or, if your copy of SAS is from ITS, insert the Solutions 2/Software 2 CD) and follow these steps:

1. Insert the CD mentioned above and click on the BUNDLES folder (or, if you're installing Version 8.1 or earlier, insert the Solutions Disk 1/Software 1 CD and click on the SAS V8 Icon, then click the BUNDLES folder).

2. Go to (click on) the EEDITOR folder.

3. Double Click the SETUP (SETUP.EXE) file and run the Setup.

Question 11: Import Wizard in SAS

When I import a table from Excel (via a *.xls file) using the Import Wizard, the data values on the first line become the variable names, whether or not the "Column Names in First Row" box in the Options dialog is checked.

How do I fix this?

A: This and other problems are often due to a mismatch between the version of the Excel *.xls file and the version specified in the Import Wizard.

For example, in Version 8.2 of SAS, if you have a Version 2002 Excel file, the highest version you can specify in the Import Wizard is 2000, and this mismatch causes SAS to ignore your choice of using or not using the first line of the Excel file for variable names.

To fix this, go back to Excel and save the *.xls file again as an older version of Excel (e.g., Excel 5 or 7), then use that same designation when using the Import Wizard in SAS.

Question 12: Installing SAS Windows 8.2

When I install SAS for Windows 8.2 (or above), one of the first questions the Setup process asks is, 'Where is the current Setinit information'. No matter what location (folder or subdirectory) I enter, it does nothing, and will not go any further.

How can I make this work?

A: As of Version 8.2, the SAS Setup requires that a valid Setinit program be available to Setup before the installation process can begin. Previously, the Setinit update was the last part of the Setup procedure.

To give SAS 8.2 and above what it needs, do the following:

1. Place the Setinit program (as provided to you in the Installation book, or on paper or in eMail by the ITS Site Coordinator) into a file in any folder you choose. This can be done by opening a new file and typing in the Setinit program, by cutting-and-pasting from email or any other method to get the valid program into a text file. (The file must be named SETINIT.SSS. The file name and folder names are not case sensitive, so you don't have to use upper case letters, but it must be spelled exactly as shown: SETINIT.SSS).

2. Begin the SAS for Windows Setup program by inserting and running the Setup CD according to the instructions in the Installation Guide.

3. When the Setup program prompts you to enter the folder (i.e., the subdirectory, or location) where the current Setinit information resides, type in the full path (folder or subdirectory name[s]) but not the file name SEINIT.SSS -- the Setup procedure should then proceed normally.

EXAMPLE:

1. Enter current Setinit information into a file called
    SETINIT.SSS in a subdirectory of the C:\ drive called
    SASTUFF.

    The full path would then look like:

    C:\SASTUFF\SETINIT.SSS

2. When the SAS Setup procedure asks what folder contains the
    current Setinit information, you type in:

    C:\SASTUFF

3. The Setup procedure should then proceed as normal.

Question 13: SAS for Windows 8.2

Is it true that SAS Version 8.2 runs under Windows NT 4.0
except if Service Pack 6 has been installed?

A: Yes. SAS for Windows Version 8.2 does not support NT
Service Pack 6. It does however; support Service Pack 6a, which
is available from Microsoft's Web site.

Question 14: SAS Data Quality-Cleanse Software

How can I install SAS Data Quality-Cleanse Software?

A: SAS Data Quality - Cleanse software is a package that was originally offered by Data Flux Corporation. This company has been acquired by SAS Institute and the software has been included in SAS for Windows as of Version 8.2.

Note that SAS Data Quality - Cleanse is a separately licensed product which currently is not part of the USC Site License.

These are the steps to install SAS Data Quality - Cleanse.

1. Install SAS for Windows as instructed in the USC installation materials.

2. 2.If SAS ask to choose the parts of the package you wish to install, choose "Select Licensed Software" (as noted in the instructions), then click the "+" sign to open the list of additional packages (some of which will be installed as part of the "Academic Computing Offer", even though they are not marked.

3. Click only the box next to SAS Data Quality - Cleanse, and then continue the install process. Software Disk 3 is no longer needed for most USC users not unless wrong choices were clicked.

4. After SAS for Windows is completely installed and clicked the SAS Data Quality - Cleanse option as noted above, that option was installed along with the original Data Flux Corporation Quality Knowledge Base (QKB), which is now out of date; the current QKB must be downloaded from the Data Flux website.

5. Click on the *.exe file that was downloaded in Step 5. Above, and this will install the new QKB

Question 15: SAS Data Sets to open automatically

I want to have SAS Data Sets (and other types of SAS files) open automatically from Windows Explorer by clicking on the icon.

How can I register these file types so that they open in this way?

A: SAS files (such as SAS Data Sets) are registered to open properly when the icon is clicked. This is done in the installation procedure.

1. If Windows loses the association between SAS and the special file types used within SAS, the file types can be re-registered.

2. Insert the SAS CD labeled "SAS Software Disk 1", and then type the following command in the Start > Run command field:

   d:\sas\setup.exe register

   Note that this example assumes that your CD drive is assigned to drive D:\ If it is assigned to a different drive letter, replace the D:\ in the example with that letter.

Question 16: Using SAS®9 for Windows

Can I use SAS®9 for Windows to directly read a file that is created by SAS®9 for UNIX?

A: Yes. You can use SAS®9 for Windows to directly read a file that is created by SAS®9 for UNIX. This is possible because starting with SAS 7 and later you can read SAS data sets without converting them between UNIX and Windows.

A translation is done behind the scenes, so you could experience performance delays. You don't have to update access, and indexes are not supported. If you cannot live with these restrictions, you should create an SAS®9 Windows file from the UNIX file.

PROC COPY with the NOCLONE option copies the UNIX data file to the native Windows format and removes the restrictions of a foreign file:

```
libname old 'path';

libname new 'path';

proc copy noclone in=old out=new;

select unix-dsname /* one level name */

run;
```

Question 17: Storing Output Delivery System (Version 7 and higher)

When using ODS LISTING in Version 7 and above, SAS doesn't recognize PROC PRINTTO (to direct Output into a file).

A: Use the undocumented FILE= option of the ODS LISTING statement to direct the output into a text file, as in the following example:

```
ODS LISTING FILE='mytest.out';
```

Question 18: Getting the Current Output

When I cut and paste (or copy and paste) results from the 'Output' window to another window (e.g., Word, Notepad), some text from a previously-cut window appears when I paste, and I can't get the current output to paste.

A: This is a known bug that happens when you highlight and cut (or copy) the last character of the current output window. If you exclude the last character of the window from your highlighting, the cut-and-paste (or copy-and-paste) will work as intended.

Question 19: Import Wizard

When using the Import Wizard (or PROC IMPORT) to import a *.xls file into an SAS Data Set, the lengths of character variables gets set to the maximum (255).

Can these lengths be modified?

A: SAS should get the lengths of character variables from the *.xls file. If this is not happening, SAS provides a downloadable patch that should correct the problem.

SAS Note SN-003583

v8.1 Import MSExcel 97/2000 Text Columns Imported with Length of 255

Using SAS 8.1/ACCESS Software for PC File Formats to read in an Excel 97/2000 text field, with PROC IMPORT or the Import Wizard, text columns are imported with a length of 255.

This behavior is fixed in the following file:

Pcff_p81.zip

Question 20: Removing Header Text from SAS Output Pages

I'd like to remove all the header information from each page of the SAS Output, and also the OBS column from PROC PRINT output.

For example, instead of:

The SAS System 1
12:12 Tuesday, January 18, 2000

```
OBS      VAR1      VAR2
 1        74        24
 2        99        41
```

I'd like to see:

```
VAR1      VAR2
 74        24
 99        41
```

A: The header information consists of three elements: TITLE ("The SAS System"), NUMBER (i.e., page number), and DATE. The TITLE is removed with a TITLE; statement -- that is, TITLE with no text specified. See example below.

The NUMBER and DATE fields are removed using an OPTIONS statement in which you specify NONUMBER and NODATE.

Here's an example:

```
data temp; input a;

cards;

6
7
;

title;

options nodate nonumber;
```

```
proc print;

run;
```

To remove the OBS column from PROC PRINT, specify NOOBS in the PROC PRINT statement, as follows:

```
proc print noobs;

run;
```

To reinstate the TITLE, run the following:

```
title 'The SAS System';
```

or any other TITLE text you prefer.

To reinstate the DATE and NUMBER text, run this:

```
options date number;
```

You can reinstate EITHER the DATE or NUMBER (but not both) by including only one of the options.

For example, to reinstate only the DATE, run this:

```
options date;
```

Question 21: Setting SAS System

When I install SAS for Windows with the intention of running most parts of the application from a CD-ROM, the SAS Setup program kicks in every time I put in the CD.

How can I set the system so that putting in the CD doesn't start the automatic setup program?

A: You can set your system's CD reader to NOT run auto start programs by clicking on the following sequence in your Windows 95 system:

Start
Settings
Control Panel
System
Device Manager
CD-ROM
Your specific CD-ROM
Properties
Settings

In this location you can un-set the 'Auto Insert Notification' feature, and the CD will no longer cause an automatic setup to happen.

Question 22: "Host Internal Error: 11" problem on SAS Icon

After clicking on the SAS icon, the burst page (opening logo) comes up, superimposed by a message box that declares a "Host Internal Error: 11" problem, then the machine freezes requiring reboot.

A: There are several possible causes for error, depending on the type of operating that you are running the SAS System under.

Host Internal Error 11 may appear on systems running Windows NT that are attempting to access datasets on Novell servers. The problem occurs when the user does not have the correct access rights, (read and write are needed). To circumvent the problem change the access rights for the user.

All Windows:

A possible cause is insufficient memory. The SAS System requires minimum of 8MB of real ram and 15MB of virtual (swap file) memory in order to correctly operate with the BASE procedures. Depending on what procedures or applications you are running, your memory requirements may be higher and will require either more real RAM or more virtual memory.

Too little free disk space is another potential error inducing condition.

This possibility would be my first guess at this point since the procedure involves multiple iterations.

Windows 3.1/95:
System resources play a big part here. Running out of file handles could possibly cause the error as could low Windows system resources. Installing Microsoft Dr. Watson program could point to some of these problems.

Question 23: Running DOS command

My programs use the 'X' command to run DOS commands from SAS, but in the current version of SAS for Windows, the X command doesn't work.

A: This could be due to a number of situations, but in general, it is a system-configuration problem. SAS has a number of documents on this topic on their website.

Another possibility is that one USC user found that his problem was because the COMSPEC parameter in his Windows 95 environment pointed to a non-existent directory, and therefore was not finding the appropriate COMMAND.COM file.

You can solve the problem by creating the directory where COMSPEC was pointing and putting COMMAND.COM in that directory, and the X command was working again. You could also change the COMSPEC pointer to point to an already-existing COMMAND.COM file.

Question 24: Page Breaks

Is there any way to make SAS output page breaks when saving the Output Window? And how can I remove the page break?

A: There are several ways to make SAS output page breaks (usually a ^L character or the equivalent), when saving the Output Window.

Here are some suggestions:

1. Use the default command line (the field on the left of the Tool Bar with the check-mark to the left of the field) then with the OUTPUT window as the active (current) window, type the PRINT command as follows:

   ```
   print file='today.out'
   ```

2. Use PROC PRINTTO as in this example:

   ```
   filename myoutput 'c:\temp\prntfils\today.out';

   proc printto print=myoutput;

   <---other SAS PROC steps-->

   proc printto;
   ```

   The final PROC PRINTTO is to turn off the redirection of the output, and return it to the Output Window.

3. Run the SAS program in batch (see examples in SAS under UNIX or SAS for Microcomputers. The .lst file that is created will have printer page breaks.

   The page break in the Output Window is controlled by the SAS System Option FORMDLIM.
   To remove the page breaks, run this:

   ```
   OPTIONS FORMDLIM=' ';
   ```

   That's single quotes with a space in between.

To turn the page break back on, run this:

```
OPTIONS FORMDLIM='';
```

That's single quotes with no space in between.

Question 25: Installation of Software on Windows

The Installation of software under Windows ran into problems.

How can I resolve this?

A: Software installation problems may be due to a conflict with other configurations of your Windows system. This document outlines a 'Safe Mode Installation'. (In Windows NT, this is referred to as 'VGA Mode'.)

This technical note describes methods for simplifying your Windows environment. Other applications or hardware drivers may interfere with the installation or execution of new software. By installing or executing in a simplified environment, it helps eliminate this possibility.

SIMPLIFYING THE ENVIRONMENT

Other applications may interfere with either the installation of software, or its execution. If you are receiving system error messages, try simplifying your environment. If you still receive error messages, reinstall the software in the simplified environment, and try running it in that environment.

The most fundamental way to simplify your Windows environment is to start the computer in Safe Mode. There are several ways to enter Safe Mode, which is described below. There are two other ways to simplify your environment. By eliminating applications from the Start Menu, and ending tasks in the Task List.

The object of simplifying your environment is to prevent other applications from interfering with software you're loading. Once you have established that, your software will install and run in a simplified environment. You can gradually introduce your previous applications, drivers, and TSR's into your start up procedure. Through this process of elimination, you can determine which applications are causing problems.

SAFE MODE

When a computer starts in Safe Mode, only basic drivers (including VGA video) are loaded.
Applications in the Start Menu are not executed. Drivers for specialized hardware, and other TSR's
are not loaded. The easiest method for entering Safe Mode is to hold down the Shift key while the machine starts up. In Windows XP, hold down the F8 key to enter Safe Mode.

Alternatively, you can enter Safe Mode through the menu screen that immediately precedes entrance into Windows itself. Occasionally, this menu is suppressed for network security reasons, though it is usually available on most Windows machines.

If you enter Safe Mode through the initial menu, you have one of three options:

1) Safe Mode (usually option 3)
2) Safe Mode with Network Support (usually option 4)
3) Step by Step Confirmation (usually option 5).

Try Safe Mode first. If you must be connected to a network, choose Safe Mode with Network Support.
If you are comfortable deciding which commands of autoexec.bat and config.sys are to be executed, you might try Step by Step Confirmation.

ELIMINATING START MENU APPLICATIONS

You may simplify your environment more selectively by eliminating applications from the Start Menu.
If an application is present in the Start Menu group, it will be loaded or executed when Windows starts up. If you suspect a particular application of causing problems, you can remove it from the menu.

To prevent applications from immediately loading upon start up, follow these menu choices: START >
SETTINGS > TASKBAR > START MENU PROGRAMS > ADVANCED >

Locate the Start Menu group, highlight its contents, and cut and paste its contents into another program group (such as Accessories). Close out all windows. Restart Windows.

To restore your original configuration, follow the menu options as described above, but instead, return applications to the Start Menu group.

CLOSE PROGRAM LIST

You may also selectively remove applications from running in the background through the Close Program
List. In general, this method is less preferred, because it ends a task that is already loaded, rather than preventing its initial loading or execution. Occasionally, a task will not release all of its resources upon termination. It is preferable to have prevent the task from loading in the first place.

You can view your Close Program List by simultaneously pressing the Control, Alt, and Delete keys.
Only press once, as multiple presses will reboot the machine.
You should now see the Close program List.
In an optimally simplified environment, only the Explorer should be running. To end other tasks, choose the task (highlight it) and then press the End Task button.

Question 26: SAS Data Set

When I click on an icon for an SAS Data Set, which is a file with an .SD2 extension, the computer tries to open the file using Sound Designer or other software, and it is difficult or impossible to recover.

A: The reason for this is that many file extensions are 'Registered' within the computer to be opened automatically by certain software packages.

First, you will need to un-register the .SD2 extension, and then re-register it with SAS.

To un-register the .SD2 extension from Sound Designer, click on 'My Computer', then click 'View', then 'Options', then click the 'File Types' tab. In the 'Registered File Types' box, scroll down to 'Sound Designer', select it, then click Remove.

To re-register the .SD2 extension as an SAS file-type, simply click on the icon for an .SD2 file, and the computer will prompt you to choose a package you want to use to open the file. When you choose SAS that should re-register the .SD2 extension to SAS for your future convenience.

Question 27: Double Space Output

Some of my output from SAS is being double-spaced. As of TS060 in Release 6.12, when PROC FREQ tries to arrange its output, if the variable names are longer than the length (format) of the variable values, it may double-space the output.

A: Since variable names in 6.12 have a maximum length of 8 characters, setting the data-value lengths to 8 fixes the problem.

EXAMPLE: Let's say VARIABL1 and VARIABL2 are being used in PROC FREQ, and the length of these variables is 4. You can determine the format length by using PROC CONTENTS.

To fix this, you would run a DATA step like the following: data new; set old; length variabl1 variabl2 8; then PROC FREQ should produce the output without additional lines.

Question 28: Proc Mixed

When I run PROC MIXED steps in succession, I get Segmentation Violations, Out of Memory messages, or other errors.

What causes these to happen?

A: Under some releases of SAS, including some maintenance levels of 6.12, PROC MIXED fails to release the memory it allocates, which causes later PROC MIXED or other steps to fail.

Here are some suggestions:

1. Increase the memory available to your SAS session using the -memory size invocation option.

    The UNIX default is 32M (megabytes), so if you're using UNIX, you might try 64M, or even higher numbers.

    It is not permitted to go above 1000M on our UNIX systems, as this may impact the work of other users. In general, it is requested that you use the minimal amount of main memory that will allow your programs to run.

    The following example shows how to invoke SAS with 48M of main memory:

    ```
    Sas  -memsize  48M
    ```

2. Run each PROC MIXED in a new SAS session, which automatically starts with all available memory.

3. The last resort, and only other alternative, is to simplify the model PROC MIXED is required to calculate.

Question 29: Renaming Entry Point in SAS 9

Can entry point names in SAS 9 be renamed or can aliases be created to match the entry names used in previous SAS versions?

A: No, in SAS 9 you cannot rename entry points or create aliases to match the entry point names that are used in previous SAS versions. Because there are architectural changes to SAS 9, such as the Threaded Kernel (TK), and there are load modules that exist that use the same name as the entry point names of previous SAS versions.

Question 30: Threaded Kernel

What is the threaded kernel, or TK?

A: Here is a description of the threaded kernel (TK) from "Architectural Changes Overview" in the Configuration Guide for SAS 9.1.3 Foundation for z/OS:

The threaded kernel (TK) is an independent internal interface to low-level OS interfaces such as memory, events, task creation, etc. The TK interface is booted one time in an address space and its services are available to any task in that address space. SAS 9.1.3 Foundation makes use of TK services. Moreover, SAS is itself initiated as a TK-created task rather than being entered directly as the job step task or via ATTACH. SAS 9.1.3 Foundation runs, in effect, as a TK application.

The introduction of TK into the SAS environment enables SAS to invoke OS services in a portable manner on multiple platforms, thereby enabling concurrent operations on multiple processors from multiple OS tasks.

Question 31: Transport Files

I've received multiple transport files because it's time-consuming to create SAS data sets from each one.

Can I write a macro to convert them, or is there a simpler method?

A: If the transport files were created with the XPORT engine, you can use PROC COPY and a wildcard reference to convert all transport files in a library to SAS data sets.

Confirm that your transport files exist in the same library and that all end with the same extension such as .xpt or .stx. In the LIBNAME statement that references the XPORT engine, substitute a wildcard for the filename.

For a code sample, see Shortcut to Importing Multiple Transport Files Created by the XPORT Engine.

For help on whether transport files were created with the XPORT engine or PROC CPORT, see FAQ 1032.

Question 32: Displaying a list of Metadata Server

Is there a way to display a listing of metadata server libraries within Base SAS software?

A: To display a listing of metadata server libraries within Base SAS software.

Follow these steps:

1. Open SAS.

2. In the command bar, type metabrowse, and select the check mark button. The Metadata Server Configuration window opens.

3. In the Metadata Server Configuration window, type the appropriate information in the Server, Port, Protocol, User Name, and Password fields, and then select 'Save' this password in your password list. Select OK. The Metadata Browser window opens.

4. In the Metadata Browser window, click the plus sign (+) beside Foundation to expand the list.

5. Navigate to SASLibrary and click the plus sign (+) to expand the list.

Question 33: Disabling Macro Prompt in Excel

How do I disable the Macro prompt in Excel when running DDE?

A: When an Excel spreadsheet that contains a macro is invoked, it will prompt you to enable the macro. Excel will stop the SAS DDE program from executing until the user responds to the prompt.

To disable the prompt, do one of the following for Excel 2000 only. You cannot do this with earlier versions of Excel.

Option 1 - Use medium security.

1. Choose security level.

    a. Select Tools>Options>Macro.
    b. Select Security Level tab and select Medium.

2. Create macros that have a digital certificate.

    a. Rerun the Microsoft Setup program.
    b. In Select Features, expand Office tools.
    c. Select Digital Signature for VBA projects and select My Computer>Run.
    d. In Windows Explorer>Office, double-click SelfCert.exe.

3. Sign the macro.

    a. Select Tools=>Macro and then select the Visual Basic Editor.
    b. In the Project explorer, select the project you want to sign
    c. Select Tools>Digital Signatures.
    d. To use the current certificate, select OK.
    e.

4. Add the source.
    a. Select Tools>Macro>Security Panel.
    b. Select Trusted Sources tab.

Option 2 - Use low security

1.   Select Tools>Options>Macro.

2.   Select Security Level tab and select Low.

Note: Use this option if your virus scanning software is very good.

Caution: selecting Low level ensures that Excel will not check for macro viruses.

For Excel 97 only

1.   Select Tools>Options.

2.   Select the General tab.

3.   Deselect the Macro Virus Protection check box.

Caution: deselecting the check box ensures that Excel will not check for macro viruses.

Question 34: Reading HTML table

How do I read HTML tables into SAS?

A: The following code can be used to import HTML tables into SAS. It uses macro code, Dynamic Data Exchange (DDE), and the IMPORT procedure to read the HTML table, and it is limited to 65,000 observations.

```
*htmlread.sas*;

*make sure you read all comments in the program fully!!!!*;

*purpose to be able to read html files into the sas system*;

*it can also create an xls file as a bonus*;

*html is limited to 65,000 observations that excel can do*;

*Access to PC file formats is required to make this run*;

*filen is the name of the html file you wish to read*;

*into the sas system*;

*filedir is the name of the directory of the html file*;

*filedir2 is the name of the directory you wish to save*;

*the xls file.  By default the xls file is the same*;

*name as the html file is*;

*row1 is a counter saying whether you have variable names*;

*in the first row of the html table you are trying to read*;

*sasname is the name of the sas dataset you are creating*;

%macro htmlread(filen,filedir,filedir2,row1,sasname);

options mprint macrogen symbolgen;

options noxwait noxsync;

data setup;

%let fullname=&filedir&filen;
%let savefile=&filedir2&filen..xls;
```

```
%let del1=call system(%unquote(%str(%'del
"&savefile"%')));

run; quit;
data setup2;

&del1;

run; quit;

/*Change the path to the install location for Excel
on your machine */

x 'c:\progra~1\micros~2\office10\excel.exe';


%put &fullname;

%let opener=%str(%'[open("&fullname")]%');

%let saveas=%str(%'[save.as("&savefile",1)]%');


/*The following DATA step gives Excel two seconds to
start */


data _null_;

x=sleep(2);

run;

quit;

filename cmds dde 'excel|system';

data _null_;

file cmds;

put %unquote(&opener);

/*----------------------------------------------------
---------*/

/* Delete the title and the top three rows */
```

```
/* You will need to modify this program as needed to
remove extraneous info from your HTML file */

/* For more information about these commands, see the
macrofun.exe Help file  */

/* You can get a copy of the macrofun.exe from
www.microsoft.com */

/*----------------------------------------------------
--------*/

put '[select("r1:r3")]';


put '[edit.delete(3)]';


*Now save the file as an excel file *;

put %unquote(&saveas);

put '[quit()]';

run;

*Now import the file as an SAS dataset from excel *;

proc import datafile="&savefile"
out=&sasname replace;

sheet="&filen";

getnames=&row1;

run; quit;

/*----------------------------------------------------
---------*/

/*Uncomment the following lines if you want the Excel
file */

/* to disappear after the program is finished */
/*----------------------------------------------------
---------*/


*data setup2;
```

```
*&del1;
*run;

*quit;

%mend htmlread;

%htmlread(print2,c:\testsas2\,c:\mysas,yes,sasuser.te
st1);
```

Question 35: Replacing the opening page break

How can I conditionally replace the opening page break when using file print?

A: The following example demonstrates how you can conditionally replace the opening page break when using the FILE PRINT statement:

```
/* Create a print file.*/

data _null_;

file 'c:\text' print;

do i=1 to 100;

put i=;

end;

 run;

/* Echo the first line to the Log to verify CC in
column 1. */

 data _null_;

infile 'c:\text' obs=1;

input;

list;

 run;

/* Now replace the page feed with a blank if present
in column 1.*/

data _null_;

infile 'c:\text' obs=1;

file 'c:\text';
```

```
input @1 char $char1.;

if char eq '0c'x then put _infile_ @1 ' ';

 run;

/* Verify change.*/

data _null_;

infile 'c:\text' obs=1;

input;
list;

run;
```

Question 36: Uninstall SAS System

How do I uninstall the SAS System for Windows V9 on the Windows operating systems?

A: Do the following Steps:

1. Click on Start --> Settings and select Control Panel and click on Add/Remove Programs.

2. Now scroll down and find SAS System for Windows V9, select this and click on Remove.

    You will see a Pop-up windows come up with a dialogue window that says Confirm File Deletion - Are you sure you want to completely remove?

3. 'SAS System for Windows V9' and all of its components? Select 'Yes' and it will proceed to Uninstall your SAS installation.

Question 37: Hiding code

Is there a way to hide my code when I execute it so that it does not appear in the log?

A: Yes, there is a way to hide your code so that it does not appear in the log. To hide your code, store it as a stored compiled macro. More importantly, the options that write information about the code to the log can be turned off in the macro. Here is a simple example:

```
libname libref 'macro-storage-library-name';

options mstored sasmstore=libref;

%macro test / store;

options nonotes nomlogic nomprint nosymbolgen
nosource nosource2;

...more SAS statements...

%mend;
```

By storing the code as a compiled macro, virtually no information about the code is written to the log. Only warnings and errors are written to the log.

For more information about the stored compiled macro facility, see SAS Macro Language Reference.
The above example is not completely foolproof, so an additional option named SECURE that can encrypt the compiled macro code is planned for a future release.

This will make it impossible to view any part of the SAS source code of the macro.

Question 38: Creating a Variable indicating a Percentile

How can I create a variable that indicates the percentile that each observation is in?

A: Use the RANK procedure that is documented in the SAS Procedures Guide for this.

For example, specify the GROUPS=100 option for percentile ranks, GROUPS=4 for quartile ranks, and GROUPS=10 for decile ranks.

The following statements create a variable, RANK_Y, which indicates the percentile values 0 to 99 that each value of the original variable, Y, falls into.

The input data set, A, is copied to the OUT= data set RANKED_A with RANK_Y included.

Note that you can create ranks for multiple variables in one run of PROC RANK. Simply list all the variables that you want to rank in the VAR statement and the names for each of the new rank variables in the RANKS statement.

If you omit the RANKS statement, then the original variable values are replaced by ranks in the OUT= data set.

```
proc rank data=a groups=100 out=ranked_a;

var y;

ranks rank_y;

run;
```

Question 39: Removing duplicates in Data Set

How can I get rid of duplicates in my SAS data set?

A: You can use PROC SORT with the NODUP or NODUPKEY option specified.

The NODUP option causes PROC SORT to compare all variable values for each observation to the previous one written to the output data set.

The NODUPKEY option causes PROC SORT to compare all BY values for each observation to those for the previous observation written to the output data set. If an exact match is found, the observation is not written to the output data set.

You can use a DATA step to accomplish the same thing, but the DATA step will allow you to output the duplicates to another file if you did not want to delete them.

In the example program below, we output the first occurrence of a BY-value to the NODUPS data set, and any duplicate values will be output to a DUPS data set. The data set OLD must be sorted by VAR1 first.

```
data dups nodups;

set old;

by var1;

if first.var1 then

output nodups;

else output dups;

run;
```

Question 40: Suppressing the automatic printing in output

How can I suppress the automatic printing of "The SAS System" at the top of my output?

A: This is the default title in Version 6 of the SAS System in batch or non-interactive mode. Turn it off by specifying TITLE;. In Version 5 of the SAS System, the default title is "SAS". It may be turned off in the same manner.

Question 41: Suppressing Page Ejects

How can I suppress page ejects between pages of procedural output?

A: If using a release prior to Release 6.06 of the SAS System, you must post process the file and remove any carriage control characters that you do not want.

If using Release 6.06 or later, specify the system option FORMDLIM=' ' to suppress page ejects.

This can be turned off by specifying FORMDLIM='', returning the FORMDLIM option to the default.

Question 42: Release 6.07

I'm working on MVS and my procedural output has carriage control characters, such as page ejects.

Why is that previous releases work fine, but Release 6.07 of the SAS System doesn't place the page ejects?

A: First, check to see if the user has set FORMDLIM=' '. In Release 6.07 and later, if a file under MVS is allocated without the carriage control attributes, that is, FB instead of FBA or VB instead of VBA, SAS does not force carriage control to the file.

In previous releases, SAS overrode the DCB characteristics and placed carriage control characters in the file.

You should allocate as VBA or FBA to receive the characters.

Question 43: Putting the value of BY Variable

How can I put the value of BY variable in a TITLE statement?

A: If using Release 6.07.03 or later of the SAS System, this can be done by using #BYVAR n and #BYVAL n inside the quoted TITLE string.

For example, the following will put the name and the value of the first BY variable on every page of output:

```
title1 'This is #BYVAR1 with a value of #BYVAL1';
```

Note that some procedures most notably PRINT and MEANS require that the NOBYLINE system option also be specified. These forces a page eject at each change of all BY variables. You can optionally specify the name of the BY variable instead of its position in the BY statement.

For example,

```
TITLE1 'This is X with a value of #BYVAL(X)';
```

Prior to Release 6.07.03, a macro generating multiple procedure steps was required.

Question 44: Converting SAS Dataset

How do I convert an SAS dataset that contains all numeric data in character variables to an SAS dataset that has numeric variables containing the numeric data with the same variable names?

A: This macro changes all the character variables within an SAS dataset to numeric.

This macro can also be easily modified to do the opposite of the above. To have all numeric variables changed to character just make the changes described within the 2 comments in the code below.

```
/** Sample dataset **/

data one;

input @1 a @3 b $10. @14 c $5. @20 d;

cards;

1 2654321234 33456 4

;

%macro vars(dsn);

%let list=;

%let type=;

%let dsid=%sysfunc(open(&dsn));

%let cnt=%sysfunc(attrn(&dsid,nvars));

%do i = 1 %to &cnt;

%let list=&list %sysfunc(varname(&dsid,&i));

%let type=&type %sysfunc(vartype(&dsid,&i));

%end;
```

```
%let rc=%sysfunc(close(&dsid));

data two(drop-

%do i = 1 %to &cnt;

%let temp=%scan(&list,&i);
_&temp

%end;);

set &dsn(rename=(

%do i = 1 %to &cnt;

%let temp=%scan(&list,&i);

&temp=_&temp

%end;));

%do j = 1 %to &cnt;

%let temp=%scan(&list,&j);

/** Change C to N for numeric to character conversion
**/

%if %scan(&type,&j) = C %then %do;

/** Also change INPUT to PUT for numeric to character
**/

&temp=input(_&temp,8.);

%end;

%else %do;

&temp=_&temp;

%end;

%end;

run;

%mend vars;
%vars(one)
```

```
/** Verify conversion has been made **/

proc contents data=two;

run;
```

Question 45: Suppress warnings in SAS Log

Can I suppress warnings in the SAS log?

A: Yes, you can. Options such as ERRORS=, NONOTES, and NOSOURCE enable you to suppress information that is written to the SAS log. However, there is not an option that turns off warnings.

If it is important that the Log window not show any information, use PROC PRINTTO or -ALTLOG to redirect the .log information to an external file.

Question 46: Checking co linearity in Logistic Regression

There is multi-co linearity among the variables in my Logistic Regression model, but PROC LOGISTIC doesn't seem to allow me to check this.

A: No co linearity diagnostics are available from PROC LOGISTIC. However, since co linearity is solely a function of the independent variables, one could use PROC REG to determine if this situation exists.

Just supply any numeric 'Y' variable and the same independent variables on the REG MODEL statement that you want to use in the LOGISTIC MODEL statement.

For example, if you're LOGISTIC code was something like:

```
PROC LOGISTIC DATA=A; MODEL OUTCOME = X1 X2 X3 X4;
RUN;
```

You could use the following REG code to investigate co linearity issues:

```
PROC REG DATA=A; MODEL ANY_Y = X1 X2 X3 X4 / TOL VIF
COLLIN; RUN;
```

Question 47: Fixing Procedures that are formatted differently

How Can I fix some procedures which results are arranged or formatted differently than in the documentation?

A: This is happening because the procedure is using a modified template to display its results.

A template is part of the Output Delivery System (ODS) and it defines the appearance of tables in the procedure's results.

To see if a user-modified template is being used, specify the ODS verify on; statement any place prior to the procedure step in question. The ODS verify off; statement turns off verification. For instance, to verify the templates used by PROC LOGISTIC:

```
ods verify on;

proc logistic;

model y = x;

run;

ods verify off;
```

If PROC LOGISTIC is using a modified template, messages similar to the following will appear in your SAS Log:

WARNING: Template STAT.LOGISTIC.PARAMETERESTIMATES was not supplied by SAS Institute!

To avoid all modified templates and use only those templates supplied by SAS Institute, specify the following statement:

```
ods path sashelp.tmplmst;
```

The templates supplied by SAS Institute are stored in SASHELP.TMPLMST. Typically, user-modified templates are stored in SASUSER.TEMPLAT. To display the locations for which SAS searches for templates, specify the following statement:

```
ods path show;
```

Question 48: SAS Site Number

How can I find my SAS Site Number?

A: If you haven't cleared your SAS log window since invoking SAS, scroll to the top of your SAS Log window. Your SAS site number appears in the first NOTE lines.

Or, you can find your SAS site number by clicking Help --> About SAS System. In the dialog box that appears, click the Site info button.

You can also display your SAS site number by executing the following SAS statement:

```
%put &syssite;
```

This prints your SAS site number in the SAS Log.

Question 49: SAS/INTRNET-Frequently asked questions and Hints

When Graphs don't show in the browser, I try adding NOCHARACTERS to the GOPTIONS statement.

Some characters are considered "unsafe" and are stripped from macro variables (and elsewhere) when they're passed from one program to another. An example of such a character is the apostrophe/single quote (').

A. Here is a possible solution, to be used with care (as apostrophes and other "unsafe" characters can cause other problems, as noted in the following).

To retain the unsafe character(s), you will need to use the APPSRV_UNSAFE function.

The left side of each assignment statement is the DATA step variable. The right side shows three different techniques for extracting the macro variable value . All of these techniques return the "safe" value of the input value. The Application Server will strip any unsafe characters (as defined by the UNSAFE option on PROC APPSRV).

This means it is usually safe to use the '&VAR' reference in Version 8 Application Dispatcher programs, unlike in previous versions. Use the appsrv_unsafe function to retrieve the full input value, including any 'unsafe' characters:

```
color=appsrv_unsafe('color')
```

There are times, such as processing free format text input, when you may want to use the original "unsafe" value for a given variable. These values may contain punctuation that would lose their meaning if the "safe" value were used. A DATA step or SCL function can be used to call to retrieve the unsafe value for a given variable.

For example, the full "unsafe" text of an input variable name MYTEXT can be accessed in a DATA step or SCL program with

APPSRV_UNSAFE: fulltext = appsrv_unsafe('MYTEXT'); A user of macro can get the value like this: %let fulltext = %sysfunc(appsrv_unsafe(MYTEXT)); If the original value does not contain unsafe characters, the value returned by the APPSRV_UNSAFE function is equal to the original value.

If the UNSAFE option is not supplied then no request values are altered and the server will function as it did in previous versions of the Application Server. (SOURCE: eMail from SAS consultant, 9 March 2004)

To begin using SAS/IntrNet, your information must be added to the main configuration file by the ITS System Group.

Cor your programs:

Choose a LIBREF (the standard SAS 'nickname', 8 characters or less)

Choose a location (subdirectory) where your programs will be stored (e.g., ~/myinetprogs/)

For your data:

Choose a LIBREF (the standard SAS 'nickname', 8 characters or less)

Choose a location (subdirectory) where your data will be stored (e.g., ~/myinetdata/)

For your formats:

Choose a LIBREF (the standard SAS 'nickname', 8 characters or less)

Choose a location (subdirectory) where your format catalogs will be stored (e.g., ~/myinetformats/)

NOTE: the data and format library can be in the same subdirectory, and use the same LIBREF if you wish.

Question 50: Accessing Auto call Macro library

How can I access the auto call macro library within SAS so I can see the macro definitions?

A: You can utilize the PC Systems when running Windows:

Click on File:Open or enter the INCLUDE command from a command line using the following path:

```
!sasroot/<prod>/sasmacro/<filename>.sas
```

or

```
!sasroot\<prod>\sasmacro\<filename>.sas
```

Where !sasroot is understood by SAS to be the location of your SAS directory (usually C:\SAS). Replace <prod> with the product name: "core" for macros supplied with base SAS, "stat" for SAS/STAT macros, "qc" for SAS/QC macros, and so on.

For example, the following statement submitted from the program editor command line copies the ADXGEN macro definition into the program editor window:

```
include '!sasroot/qc/sasmacro/adxgen.sas'
```

Systems running UNIX:

Click on File:Open or enter the INCLUDE command from a command line using the following path:

```
!sasroot/sasautos/<filename>.sas
```

Where !sasroot is understood by SAS to be the location of your SAS directory. For example, the following statement submitted from the program editor command line copies the ADXGEN macro definition into the program editor window:

```
include '!sasroot/sasautos/adxgen.sas'
```

Mainframe Systems (MVS and VM/CMS):

Click on File:Open-->Read file... or enter the INCLUDE command from a command line using the following file specification:

```
sasautos(<filename>)
```

For example, the following statement submitted from the program editor command line copies the ADXGEN macro definition into the program editor window:

```
include sasautos(adxgen)
```

VAX Systems running VMS:

Enter the INCLUDE command from a command line using the following file specification:

```
sasautos(<filename>)
```

For example, the following statement submitted from the program editor command line copies the ADXGEN macro definition into the program editor window:

```
include sasautos(adxgen)
```

Macintosh Systems:

Click on File-->Open, or enter the INCLUDE command from a command line using the following path:

In Release 6.12 of SAS, select File-->Open, or type INCLUDE and the following command on a command line:

```
include: !saspath:auto:<filename>.sas
```

Where !saspath is the location of your SAS folder. For example, the following statement when submitted from the command line in the Program Editor copies the ADXGEN macro definition into the Program Editor window:

```
include '!saspath:auto:adxgen.sas'
```

Question 51: Accessing Sample Library Programs

How can I access the sample library programs?

A: You can access the sample library programs from within SAS software as follows:

PC Systems Running Windows:

In SAS 9, select Help->SAS Help and Documentation, and on the Contents tab in the left pane, select Learning to Use SAS->SAS Sample Programs.

In SAS 7 and SAS 8, select Help->SAS System Help. Select Sample SAS Programs and Applications in the right pane or use the Contents tab in the left pane. Prior to SAS 7, select Help->Sample Programs.

You can also access the sample programs directly via the include command using this path:

```
!sasroot/<prod>/sample/<filename>.sas
```

or

```
!sasroot\<prod>\sample\<filename>.sas
```

Where !sasroot is understood by SAS to be the location of your SAS directory (usually C:\SAS). Replace <prod> with the SAS product name (for example, stat, iml, qc, and so on). For samples in Base SAS software, replace <prod> with core. For example, the following statement that is submitted from the SAS command line copies the GEOMEAN.SAS file into the Program Editor window:

```
include '!sasroot/core/sample/geomean.sas'
```

Systems Running UNIX

In SAS 7 or later, select Help->SAS System Help. From the Contents tab, navigate to the Sample SAS Programs and Applications page and then to the SAS product that you want. Prior to SAS 7, select Help->Sample Programs. You can also access the sample programs directly via File->Open or the include command using this path:

```
!sasroot/samples/<prod>/<filename>.sas
```

Where !sasroot is understood by SAS to be the location of your SAS directory (usually C:\SAS).

Replace <prod> with the SAS product name (for example, stat, iml, qc, and so on).

For samples in Base SAS software, replace <prod> with core. For example, the following statement that is submitted from the SAS command line copies the GEOMEAN.SAS file into the Program Editor window:

```
include '!sasroot/core/sample/geomean.sas'
```

Mainframe Systems (MVS and VM/CMS)

Contact your SAS site representative to find out the location of the SAS sample library.

For example, if the sample library is located in SAS.SAS82.SAMPLE, the following statement that is submitted from the Program Editor command line copies the GEOMEAN file into the Program Editor window:

```
include 'sas.sas82.sample(geomean)'
```

VAX Systems Running VMS:

In SAS 7 or later, select Help->SAS System Help. From the Contents tab, navigate to the Sample SAS Programs and Applications page and then to the SAS product that you want. Prior to SAS 7, select Help->Sample Programs.

You can also access the sample programs directly via File->Open or the include command using this path:

```
SAS$SAMPLES:[<prod>]<filename>.sas
```

Replace <prod> with the SAS product name (for example, stat, iml, qc, and so on). For samples in Base SAS software, replace <prod> with core. For example, the following statement that is submitted from the SAS command line copies the GEOMEAN.SAS file into the Program Editor window:

```
include 'sas$samples:[core]geomean.sas'
```

Macintosh Systems

You can access the sample programs via File->Open or the include command using this path:

```
!saspath:sample:<prod>:<filename>.sas
```

Where !saspath is understood by SAS to be the location of your SAS folder. Replace <prod> with the product name (for example, stat, iml, qc, and so on).

For samples in Base SAS software, replace <prod> with core. For example, the following statement that is submitted from the SAS command line copies the GEOMEAN.SAS file into the Program Editor window:

```
include '!saspath:sample:core:geomean.sas'
```

Question 52: Experimental Software

What does it mean for software to be "Experimental"?

A: The Experimental Software designation often refers to a preliminary version of software that is released in order to get user feedback.

While experimental software has been tested before its release, it has not received the level of testing that SAS deems necessary for software to be called "production."

The design and syntax of experimental software is likely to change before its production release.
However, experimental software might be included as part of a production product.

Whenever you use an experimental procedure, statement, or option, a message prints to the SAS log indicating that the procedure, statement, or option is designated as being experimental.

You should always check for any known problems in the SAS Notes when using experimental software.

Question 53: Creating an Output Data Set

How can I create an output data set from a specific table or write a particular statistic that is displayed by a procedure to a data set?

A: Beginning with SAS 7, you can use the ODS OUTPUT statement to create a data set from any table that is created by any procedure. The ODS OUTPUT statement is a global statement, so it can be placed anywhere before the termination of the procedure. Here is the form of the ODS OUTPUT statement:

```
ods output <table-name> = <data-set-name>;
```

To create a data set from a given table, you need first to find the name of the table. If you specify the following statement before your procedure statements, then the displayed output will show each table name immediately before the table is displayed:

```
ods trace on / listing;
```

You can turn off the listing of table names by using the following statement:

```
ods trace off;
```

The following statements add the table names to the displayed output of PROC REG:

```
ods trace on / listing;

proc reg;

model y = x;

run;

ods trace off;
```

Note that most procedures have an "ODS Table Names" section in their documentation that lists the names of the tables that the procedure can create.
If you want to write the parameter estimates table from PROC REG to a data set, you must first know the table name. The ODS TRACE statement or the "ODS Table Names" section of the PROC REG documentation shows you that the table name is ParameterEstimates. To create a data set named PARMS from this table, specify the following statements:

```
ods output ParameterEstimates=parms;
proc reg;

model y = x;

run;
```

Question 54: Services from Statistical Technical Support

What services can I expect from Statistical Technical Support at SAS?

A: Here are the responsibilities of Statistical Technical Support:

1. Direct customers to the appropriate SAS procedure for the particular type of analysis that they request. It is the customer's responsibility to determine which type of analysis is appropriate for their needs.

2. Answer questions concerning specific details of the statistical procedures, such as discussing available options and limitations.

3. Provide references for formulas and statistical techniques used by our algorithms where possible.

4. Provide the customer with limited guidance and references for interpreting the output produced by the statistical procedures.

5. Investigate reported problems in our software and pass those which we verify on to the software development team for response.

6. Provide limited and general statistical advice as we deem necessary on a case-by-case basis.

Due to limited knowledge of any particular customer's data analysis situation, it cannot provide general statistical consulting services such as selection of statistical methodology or design of experiments.

Nor can we provide customized SAS code (for example, CONTRAST, ESTIMATE, or TABLES statements) for a customer's particular needs.

Question 55: Sensitivity Analysis

Is there a procedure to do Sensitivity Analysis?

A: Sensitivity Analysis is a broad method that can be applied to virtually any statistical method and therefore any SAS procedure or program.

For example, you want to find out how sensitive the fit of your regression model is to a change in the nature of one or more of the predictors. Or you might want to see how much the results of a specialized program you wrote in SAS/IML change as you change inputs.

Because of this broad applicability, the capability of SAS to do sensitivity analysis is not confined to a single procedure. Rather, the SAS language provides many components that you can use to conduct a sensitivity analysis.

For example, using the random number generators and other capabilities in the DATA step and/or the experimental design construction capabilities in SAS/QC software, you can construct data sets covering a range of scenarios or assumptions about the underlying phenomenon under study.

You can run the desired statistical procedure or program on each of these data sets in turn and then output the statistics whose sensitivity is of interest.

Note that you can use the ODS OUTPUT statement to output any table produced by any procedure to a data set for further processing.

Finally, you can use any of our statistical procedures to summarize the behavior of the relevant statistics.

Question 56: Procedures for Analysis Survey Data Base

Are there any procedures for the analysis of survey data based on complex sampling designs?

A: Yes, beginning with Version 7, SAS/STAT software includes several procedures for survey data analysis:

* PROC SURVEYSELECT provides a variety of methods for selecting probability-based random samples as well as samples according to a complex multistage design that includes stratification, clustering, and unequal probabilities of selection.

* PROC SURVEYMEANS computes estimates of survey population totals and means, estimates of their variances, confidence limits, and other descriptive statistics.

* Beginning with SAS 9.1, PROC SURVEYFREQ produces one-way to n-way frequency and cross tabulation tables for survey data. These tables include estimates of totals and proportions (overall, row percentages, and column percentages) and the corresponding standard errors.

* PROC SURVEYREG performs regression analysis for sample survey data, fitting linear models and computing regression coefficients and the covariance matrix.

* Beginning with SAS 9.1, PROC SURVEYLOGISTIC performs logistic regression on data that arises from a survey sampling scheme. Variances of the regression parameters and odds ratios are computed using a Taylor expansion approximation.

The SURVEYMEANS, SURVEYFREQ, SURVEYREG, and SURVEYLOGISTIC procedures can incorporate survey sample designs including designs with stratification, clustering, and unequal weighting.

Question 57: Alternative Methods for Neural Networks

Are there any alternative methods for using neural networks within SAS?

A: Here are some possibilities to consider:

*Second- and higher-order neural nets are linear models or generalized linear models with interaction terms. They can be implemented directly with the GENMOD, GLM, or RSREG procedures in SAS/STAT software.

*Functional-link nets are linear models or generalized linear models that include various transformations of the predictor variables. They can be implemented with SAS/STAT PROC TRANSREG or with a DATA step to do the transformations, followed by the GENMOD, GLM, LOGISTIC, or REG procedure in SAS/STAT.

*AVQ (Adaptive Vector Quantization) is a class of non convergent algorithms for least-squares cluster analysis. Better results can be obtained with PROC FASTCLUS or PROC CLUSTER in SAS/STAT.

*Probabilistic neural nets are identical to kernel discriminant analysis which can be done with the METHOD=NPAR option in SAS/STAT PROC DISCRIM.

*General regression neural nets are identical to Nadaraya-Watson kernel regression.

Question 58: Reading SAS Date values (and other numeric data) from a string variable

How does one give a date value in a readable format to a new variable in an assignment statement?

When I try something like 01-15-93 (January 15, 1993), SAS evaluates the numbers as if it were an arithmetic expression.

A: First, create a new variable (you can DROP it right away, as it is only used during the current step) that reads '01-15-93' as an alphanumeric string, then use the INPUT function to read that string into a new variable.

EXAMPLE
=======
The first assignment statement creates temporary string variable X that contains the date string, and then the second assignment statement creates the 'real' variable DATE using the INPUT statement to input X with an INFORMAT of MMDDYY8.

The variable A is INPUT only to show how regular data can be INPUT in the same step with an assignment statement.

```
data temp; input a; drop x;

x='07-11-46';              /*<-- first assignment
statement   */

date=input(x,mmddyy8.);    /*<-- second assignment
statement */
cards;

5
4
6
7
5
;

proc print; format date date.;    run;
```

Question 59: "n equations"

How can I solve a system of n equations in n unknowns?

A: For estimation of a linear system of simultaneous equations using either two- or three-stage least squares, use SAS/ETS PROC SYSLIN with the 2SLS or 3SLS option in the PROC SYSLIN statement.

For estimation of a nonlinear system of simultaneous equations using either two- or three-stage least squares, use the SAS/ETS PROC MODEL with the 2SLS or 3SLS option in the FIT statement.

For a system of linear or nonlinear equations, the SOLVE statement in SAS/ETS PROC MODEL can be used to obtain the unknowns. The equations must be specified in general form and starting values for each unknown should be provided in an input data set.

The following example illustrates how to solve N nonlinear equations in N unknowns:

```
/**********************************************************/
* This sample job illustrates how to solve a system of nonlinear
-* equations using PROC MODEL.  The equations to solve are:
*
*      x1 + x2 - x1*x2 = -2
*      x1 * exp(-x2)  = 1
/**********************************************************
/
data init;   ** supply initial values **;

x1=.2; x2=-2;

run;
proc model data=init;
eq.one = x1 + x2 - x1*x2 + 2;
eq.two = x1 * exp(-x2) - 1;
solve x1 x2/itprint out=solved outpredict;

run;
proc print data=solved;
```

```
run;
```

Question 60: Creating Design Matrix in a Data Set

How can I create the corresponding design matrix (dummy, indicator, or design variables) in a data set?

A: If you know the model, there are three methods for creating a data set that contains the design matrix:

You can use an ODS OUTPUT statement with PROC GLMMOD to create a data set from the design matrix that is used in PROC GLM. Specify the model in the MODEL statement and identify any categorical predictors in the CLASS statement.

Note that PROC GLMMOD only offers indicator (or dummy) coding of categorical predictor variables.

For example, the GLM statements below fit the indicated model and the GLMMOD statements that follow create a data set from the same design matrix that was used in PROC GLM.

Use the ODS LISTING statements if you want to suppress display of the GLMMOD output in the Output window.

```
proc glm data=a;

class a b c;

model y=a b c a*b;

run;

ods output designpoints=xmatrix;

ods listing close;

proc glmmod data=a;

class a b c;

model y=a b c a*b;

run;
```

```
ods listing;
```

Beginning with SAS 9, you can also use the OUTDESIGN= and OUTDESIGNONLY options in PROC LOGISTIC. PROC LOGISTIC can create design variables by using any of several different coding methods (parameterizations) including indicator (dummy) coding, effects coding, polynomial coding, and others. Specify the model in the MODEL statement and identify any categorical predictors in the CLASS statement. Use the PARAM= option in the CLASS statement to select the coding method.

The following statements create a data set from the same design matrix as produced above by PROC GLMMOD (and internally by PROC GLM):

```
proc logistic data=a outdesign=xmatrix outdesignonly;

class a b c / param=glm;

model y=a b c a*b;
run;
```

But you can also use other coding methods. For example, these statements use effects coding for the categorical (CLASS) variables:

```
proc logistic data=a outdesign=xmatrix outdesignonly;

class a b c / param=effect;

model y=a b c a*b;

run;
```

See the LOGISTIC documentation for information about the various coding methods that are available.

You can also use PROC TRANSREG. It offers both indicator and effects coding methods. Specify any categorical variables in the CLASS expansion. Use the ZERO= option to select a reference category or, as below, ZERO=NONE to obtain the less-than-full-rank coding that is used by PROC GLM.

Specify any continuous predictors, the response, and any other variables that you want transferred to the output data set in the ID statement.

For example, the following statements create a data set from the same design matrix as produced above by PROC GLMMOD (and internally by PROC GLM):

```
proc transreg data=a design;

model class(a b c a*b / zero=none);

id y;

output out=xmatrix;

run;
```

 Effects coding can be done as follows:

```
proc transreg data=a design;

model class(a b c a*b / effects);

id y;

output out=xmatrix;

run;
```

Note that PROC TRANSREG automatically creates a macro variable, &_trgind, which contains a list of variable names that it creates. You can use this macro variable in subsequent procedures to refer to the full model.

Question 61: Character-to-Numeric Conversions and Numeric-to-Character Conversions

How can I convert a character variable to a numeric variable and a numeric variable to a character variable?

A: This can be solved with an assignment statement in a DATA step and, in the case of Numeric-to-Character conversions, a LENGTH statement or the equivalent to create the new Character variable.

Before examples, it may help to clarify a few terms. SAS has two types of variables: Character and Numeric. They are stored in different ways, so SAS can not always use them both in all situations. For example, calculations such as a mean or standard deviation cannot be done using a Character variable, even if all the values appear to be numbers.

You would know if SAS has stored a variable as Character or Numeric when you use PROC PRINT, if a variable is Character, the values will be left-justified by default, since SAS regards them simply as text.

For example

4
8.247
0.56
98

If the same values are stored in a Numeric variable, the values will be right-justified (with trailing zeroes added as required to fit the format dimensions:

4.000
8.247
0.560
98.000

The more certain method of determining if a variable is Character or Numeric is to run PROC CONTENTS, as follows:

```
proc contents data=new;
run;
```

The output from this PROC will list the variables alphabetically in a table, and the column titled "Type" will have either a "Num" or "Char" label for each variable.

Character-to-Numeric Variable Conversions

```
existing (character) variable: ageold

desired (numeric) variable: agenew
data new; set old;

agenew=input(ageold, 8.0);
```

The 8.0 specification is the numeric format for the new variable. Any valid numeric format can be specified, but note that if you use one that specifies decimals, such as 8.2, the numbers in the string variable will be read into the lowest decimal category that the format specifies.

For example, with the 8.0 format, 5 (character) becomes 5.0 (number), but with the 8.2 format, 5 (character) becomes 0.05 (number). By the same token, however, with the 8.2 format, 5.23 (character) becomes 5.23 (number), because the original character value has an imbedded decimal, which SAS respects.

An alternative method of converting a Character variable into a Numeric (assuming all values are valid numbers) is the simple technique of multiplying by "1" as in this example:

```
data new; set old;

agenew=1*ageold;
```

While this technique will give the desired results, SAS Institute programmers and other sophisticated SAS users regard it to be not as elegant as the solution (above) that uses the INPUT function. In other words, if you use this technique, you may risk labeling yourself as a "novice" (but, like many novices, you will probably get the results you want!).

Numeric-to-Character Variable Conversions

```
existing (numeric) variable: oldgroup

desired (character) variable: newgroup
```

When creating a new character variable, you need to define (declare) the variable before doing the conversion. This can be done easily with the LENGTH statement, though other methods such as the ATTRIB statement work equally well.

NOTE that because of the left-justification of string variables and the right-justification of numeric variables, it is always a good idea to make the width (format) of the string variable at least as wide as the widest numeric value in your data, and to add the LEFT function to the equation so that the values will be left-justified, like Character variables that SAS creates from "scratch" (e.g., in INPUT statements):

```
data new; set old; length newgroup $ 12
newgroup=left(oldgroup);
```

The dollar-sign ($) tells SAS that the NEWGROUP variable should be initialized as a Character variable, and the 12 gives that variable a (maximum) length of 12 bytes.

Note that if you have any numeric values that are longer than the format length that you specify [including any decimal point], you must use a LENGTH value at least as long as the longest number, or the values will be truncated. Conversely, if you're longest value is going to be, say, 6 characters [including decimal point], there is no need to use a format width greater than 6).

Question 62: Launching SAS under UNIX

When I try to invoke SAS under UNIX, I get error messages and SAS doesn't come up.

How can I resolve this?

A: The basic requirement is that you have a correct terminal type and that UNIX be able to find the SAS command. Also, UNIX may have set the DISPLAY environment variable incorrectly for your terminal emulation. If these are not set up properly, SAS may fail. Another problem that arises occasionally is that one's profile.sct01 file gets corrupted.

Here are some error messages and possible solutions for these problems.

* Incorrect terminal type -- the SAS Display Manager windows will be misaligned or lined with non-ASCII characters instead of solid lines, or the screen will simply look like garbage.

Fix this by setting the terminal type to one that SAS can use properly. Usually this will be vt100, but others may be more appropriate in some situations. Here's a short list:

```
set term=vt100
```

* UNIX can't find SAS command -- after typing sas you'll get the message sas: command not found

Fix this by sourcing the setup file, which adds SAS to your existing path.

```
source /usr/usc/sas/default/setup.csh
```

* permission denied -- (rude, isn't it!) after typing sas you'll get the message permission denied

This probably means that you're logged in to a machine where SAS is not licensed to run. For example, in the ITS User Rooms when you log into a Sun Workstation, you are logged into the local machine, even though your file structure still resides (and appears to originate from) aludra.

Fix this by remote-logging into aludra:

```
rlogin   aludra
```

And then proceed as usual (i.e., set the terminal type if you need to, source the setup file, etc., as documented in SAS for UNIX, and then start SAS).

li>Incorrect DISPLAY environment variable setting -- most users of SAS for UNIX connect in an ASCII (or character-based) window, e.g., when using Telnet from home or from a User Room microcomputer. Sometimes, UNIX queries the terminal and sets the DISPLAY environment variable to the local machine name or IP number.

When SAS sees this, it may try to open SAS in X Windows mode, which an ASCII (or character-based) terminal can not handle. The result is an error message such as:

ERROR: Cannot open X display. Check display name/server access authorization.

Usually, this can be fixed by unsetting the DISPLAY variable:

```
unsetenv   DISPLAY
```

* profile.scto1 file gets corrupted -- SAS may not open if something has happened to the user's profile.
The profile is actually an SAS catalog file (.scto1) where user modifications, if any, get stored when users customize things such as key settings, window position, or a number of other possible customizations.

Many users don't ever touch their profile files, and these files don't get corrupted often, but it is not unusual.

One error message that you might see when the profile has been corrupted is:
ERROR: Segmentation Violation captured in task 'SASXKERN'.

FORCED TERMINATION: module
`/612/master/UNIX/src/vtdelet.c':

Task deletion in critical region:

Sometimes different messages also indicate a corrupted profile.sct01 file.

SAS always checks a user's sasuser/ subdirectory for a file called profile.sct01 when it starts up.
If none exists, SAS creates a new (vanilla) one. By default, sasuser/ is a subdirectory of your home (~/) directory.

If you have not modified any features of SAS and most users do not do any modifications, simply rename (or remove) your profile file, and when SAS starts up again it will create a new, vanilla profile for you that is not corrupted. To make this happen, do the following:

```
cd  ~/sasuser

mv  profile.sct01  profile.old

sas
```

When SAS starts up again, you will have a clean, uncorrupted profile file. If you have modified key settings, window configurations, colors or any other settings that are stored in the profile it is a good idea to make a copy of that file (each time you modify it) in case it gets corrupted in the future.

If you have a copy of your last-modified profile.sct01 file, you will not have to re-establish all the settings that were saved there if the file gets corrupted. To make a copy of your profile, do the following:

```
cd  ~/sasuser
cp  profile.sct01  profile.permanent
```

If your modified profile file gets corrupted, you can then restore it as follows:

```
cd  ~/sasuser
cp  profile.permanent  profile.sct01
```

Question 63: Exporting SAS Dataset

How do I export my SAS dataset to a specific sheet name in Excel?

A: Beginning with Release 8.1 of SAS/ACCESS to PC File Formats, the sheet name in the specified workbook will have the same name as the SAS dataset.

For example:

```
PROC EXPORT DATA= SASUSER.CATEGORIES

OUTFILE= "c:\temp\test.xls"

DBMS=EXCEL2000 REPLACE;

RUN;
```

This code creates a sheet that is named CATEGORIES in the TEST.XLS workbook.

Note: You cannot "add" the sheet to an existing workbook. You can use the DATASETS procedure to rename a dataset prior to exporting.

For example:

```
PROC DATASETS LIBRARY=SASUSER MT=DATA NOLIST;

CHANGE CATEGORIES=CATS;

QUIT;
```

Question 64: SAS/Access to Oracle

I'm using SAS\ACCESS to ORACLE. Why am I getting this:

ERROR: Oracle CONNECT Error: ORA-12154: TNS:could not resolve service name?'

A: This error usually occurs because the PATH statement is set incorrectly. The PATH statement that is used in Proc Access, Proc Dbload and Proc Sql Pass-thru is the Oracle connect string which is defined in the TNSNAMES.ORA file.

When using Proc Access and Proc Dbload, the PATH statement must begin with an @ sign.

For example:

```
Path='@connect_string';
```

Question 65: SAS/Access Interface to PC File Formats

How can I tell if SAS/ACCESS Interface to PC File Formats is installed on my machine?

A: Browse to !sasroot\access\sasexe. Look for files sasimoda.dll, sasimxls.dll, sasimwkn.dll, or sasimdbf.dll. If you do not see these DLLs listed, then you do not have this product installed.

Question 66: Using SAS Data Sets with *.sd7 extensions in Version 9

I have some SAS Data Sets with the file extension *.sd7 and SAS for Windows Version 9.x doesn't recognize them.

A: Some versions of SAS for Windows have used *.sd7 as the extension for SAS Data Sets to provide compatibility with older versions of DOS that allowed only 3-character extensions.

To use these SAS Data Sets in Version 9.x and up of SAS, simply change the extension from *.sd7 to *.sas7bdat. This is done outside of SAS, using Windows Explorer, the "My Computer" shortcut, or a Command Prompt window.

Question 67: Determining Schema

How do I determine the SCHEMA for my table(s) using SAS/ACCESS to OLE DB?

A: To determine the SCHEMA that is associated with a particular table or tables using SAS/ACCESS to OLE DB, you can submit the following code.

When submitted, the SAS data set called WORK.TABS will contain a list of all tables the user has access to via OLE DB and the corresponding SCHEMA associated with each table:

```
proc sql;

connect to oledb;

create table tabs as select table_schema table_name

from connection to oledb (OLEDB::Tables);

quit;
```

Question 68: Setting Program Editor Colors in SAS under UNIX

How can I set a program editor color in SAS under UNIX?

A: Some displays show colors in the SAS Program Editor that make the text difficult to read (light yellow on white, for example).

The text colors can be changed using the Tools menu in the Program Editor Window. If you don't have the menu bar with "Tools" in it, you can get the menu by typing pmenu at your command line.

Sometimes this must be typed twice before it works! To reinstate your command line after working with the Program Editor Modification window, click Tools > Options > Turn Command Line On;

Click:

Tools > Options > Program Editor > Appearance

Make sure the box next to "Display SAS Code in Color" is checked, then click "Modify" and you'll be able to change the colors to your specifications, while viewing some sample code in the dialog box.

To save your color (or other) choices for future sessions, type wsave at your command line in the Program Editor window; or, if you are using the menus (and have no command line), type wsave in the command line of the SAS ToolBox the command field with the check-mark box to the left of it. Remember if you use the SAS ToolBox command line that the Program Editor window must be the active (last-visited) window in order for the wsave command to be applied to it.

Question 69: Finding your IP address when Using SAS for UNIX under Micro-X or Mac-X

I'm connecting to UNIX through X-Windowing software such as XWin32 (Windows) or Mac-X (Macintosh) and the software I'm planning to use requires an X-windowing environment (and/or I may want to generate graphs), but I don't know how to set the DISPLAY environment variable.

A: The DISPLAY environment variable needs to be set to display graphical output on your local machine. The syntax is:

```
UNIX Prompt>   setenv   DISPLAY   <machinename>:0
```

Where "machinename" is the name or IP number of your machine. (Almost always you will have no machine name, so you will use the IP number.)

To determine your IP number, do one of the following:

- For Windows NT

  Click on Start>Programs>Command Prompt, then type: IPCONFIG

- For Windows 95 or Windows 98

  Click on Start>Programs>Command Prompt (or MS-DOS Prompt), then type: WINIPCFG

- For Macintosh OS X

  Click: Apple Menu>System Preferences>Network>TCP/IP. The IP address will be shown in the middle of the box

- On Any System

  In your WWWeb browser, enter the URL: http://www.usc.edu/whoami

Question 70: Launching SAS for UNIX in an X-Win session in the ITS Public User Areas

How Can I use the X-Windowing PC client in the USC user rooms?

A: The PCs in the ITS-supported public user rooms have an Applications Launcher that appears to the right once you log in. For detailed information on how to set up the X Win client, click the X-Win Setup document link. The information in this link is summarized below.

To begin the process, click the X-Win Config link, then proceed as follows:

Click the "Wizard" button in the X-Win Configuration Window

Click the "rexec" entry in the Connect Method box

Enter aludra.usc.edu (or the name of the host you're connecting to) in the field called "Host Name"

Enter your Login Name and Password in the respective fields

Choose "SunOS (Solaris)" from the Host Type pull-down and in the Command field, you should see the following:

```
/usr/openwin/bin/xterm -ls -display $MYIP:$DNUM
```

If that command doesn't work, you can use:

```
/usr/usc/X11/bin/xterm -display $MYIP:0.0
```

$MYIP is a symbolic variable that should resolve to the IP number assigned for that session to your PC.

Enter a nickname in the Name of Session box; it can be any text, but it's recommended for consistency that you use the name of the host you're logging into, perhaps followed by a number (e.g., aludra1)

If you want to launch your X-win session immediately (usually recommended), click the box next to "Launch this session now".

If you don't click the box next to "Launch this session now" you can click the blue "X" icon in the Windows task bar (usually at the bottom right of the screen) to bring up your X-Win session window; when you click the blue "X" icon, this will bring up a button with the nickname of your session in it, and then you click that button.

If you want to revise the settings you've entered above, you can click the "X-Win Config" link, and then click the Wizard button to repeat the steps.

Click on the "Display" tab in the Wizard, and set the appropriate IP address for your local computer. (i.e., the computer you are using in the Lab). Your IP number should be the one in the list that begins with 128.125.

Usually the steps above will be sufficient, and you will be able to run X-Windowing applications without any further settings.

It is possible, however, that once the X-Win session window opens, you may need to set the DISPLAY environment variable to display at your local machine (i.e., your local IP number).

To determine your local IP number, open an MS-DOS or Command Prompt Window (this is usually done by clicking on Start>Programs>Accessories>Command Prompt), and type the command ipconfig; this will give you the IP number next to the words, "IP Address"; enter that number in the following command at your UNIX prompt:

```
setenv DISPLAY <your IP number>:0.0
```

For example, if your IP number is 128.125.999.888, you would enter

```
setenv DISPLAY 128.125.999.888:0.0
```

Your chosen X-Windows software package (e.g., SPSS for UNIX, SAS for UNIX, etc.) should now start up correctly.

Question 71: Sending an SAS Dataset through e-mail

How can I transfer the SAS Dataset to someone thru e-mail?

A: You can do it between UNIX systems. SAS Data Sets that have been converted into transport files can be transferred via e-mail provided they are uuencoded.

Here are the steps.

On the sending operating system:

1. Create a transport file using either PROC CPORT (preferred) or PROC COPY (if the receiving system requires this).

2. Create a uuencoded version of the Transport file using UUENCODE:

    ```
    uuencode  trans.file  label  >  out.file
    ```

    where trans.file is the path/name of the SAS transport file.

    label- the label argument is required.

    It is included in the encoded file's header as the name of the file into which uudecode is to place the binary (encoded) data.

    out.file- is the path/name of the newly created uuencoded file.

3. Include out.file in the e-mail message.

    NOTE: Some e-Mailers encode attachments automatically using BinHex or similar devices; if your e-Mailer has this feature, you may not need the above instructions to send an encoded SAS data set.

On the receiving operating system:

1. Un-encode the file received via e-mail using UUDECODE.

    ```
    uudecode   message.file
    ```

    Where message.file is the file saved from e-mail.

    The un-encoded file will be an SAS transport file with the
    name given to it in the uuencode process.

2. Using PROC CIMPORT (or PROC COPY if the original
    transport file was made with PROC COPY), convert the
    transport file back into an SAS Data Set. (Documentation for
    PROC CPORT, PROC CIMPORT and PROC COPY is in the
    SAS Manuals.

    And then choose any of several links in the "SAS Across
    Different Systems" section.

Between Microcomputers:

SAS data sets created in SAS for Windows or SAS for Macintosh.
Sometimes (please note the implied stress on *sometimes*) can
be sent as-is through e-Mail to be used on other microcomputers
without corruption of the data. Since there are so many e-Mail
programs and procedures available today, it is not possible to
predict or summarize their performance here. Trial and error is
recommended.

In any case, it is always more reliable to make an SAS Transport

File first. It is not advisable to compress the file, as each step of
conversion, compression, or e-Mail transfer has some potential
for corruption of the data. Simple conversion to a transport file
within SAS and then e-Mailing that transport file to the recipient
should work fine.

The best way, whenever possible, to move SAS data from one
microcomputer to another is on a diskette or Zip disk. No
translation or conversion takes place and the only variable in the
process is the U.S. Mail or other delivery service.

Question 72: Size of an SAS Data Set

I want to create an SAS data set from a raw data and I want to know how large the SAS data set will be?

A: The formula for calculating the size of an SAS data set is:

```
(218 + (v*106)) + (nobs*(tvl + 4))
```

Where v is the number of variables, nobs is the number of observations, and tvl is the total of all variable lengths.

For example, suppose you have a data set with 2 variables (v=2), each of which has a length of 8 (tvl=16), and 10 observations (nobs=10). The size of the data set is (218 + (2*106)) + (10*(16 + 4)) = 628 bytes

SAS stresses the point that this is a guideline, not an absolute formula.

This does not allow one to calculate the potential size of an SAS data set from the size (in bytes) of raw data files. There is probably no way to estimate accurately simply from the size of the raw data file.

Question 73: Writing SAS Data Set into Raw Data

How can I write out a data from my SAS Data Set to a raw data file?

A: Do the following:

1. Enter a LIBNAME statement that tells SAS where the OLD library is, for example:

```
LIBNAME   OLD   'C:\SASDATA'; ***Windows or SAS-PC
example;

LIBNAME   OLD   '~/SASDATA'; ***UNIX example;
```

2) Enter a FILENAME statement which points to a UNIX or DOS file to hold the output raw data, as in these examples:

```
FILENAME   nikname   'C:\RAWDATA\MYOUT.RAW';
***Windows or SAS-PC;

FILENAME   nikname   '~/rawdata/myout.raw';
***UNIX;
```

2. Then add this basic program after your LIBNAME and FILENAME statements:

```
DATA new;

SET old.sasdata;

FILE nikname;

PUT @ VAR1 @ VAR2 ... @ VARn;

RUN;
```

Where the @'s in the PUT statement followed by a column number "point" to those specific columns. For example,

```
PUT @1 VAR1 @5 VAR2;
```

Would place VAR1 beginning in column 1 and VAR2 would start in column 5.

The FILE statement directs the 'output' from the PUT statement into the file referenced by 'nickname', which is where you will find your raw data when this program is finished.

Here are two complete examples, based on the programs above:

UNIX

```
LIBNAME   OLD   '~/SASDATA';

FILENAME   nikname   '~/rawdata/myout.raw';
DATA new;

SET old.sasdata;
FILE nikname;
PUT @1 VAR1 @5 VAR2;

RUN;
```

Windows/SAS-PC (DOS)

```
LIBNAME   OLD   'C:\SASDATA';

FILENAME   nikname   'C:\RAWDATA\MYOUT.RAW';

DATA new;

SET old.sasdata;

FILE nikname;

PUT @1 VAR1 @5 VAR2;

RUN;
```

Question 74: Garbage Characters in SAS for Windows Output files

My SAS for Windows (6.11 and higher) output file looks like garbage when I move it to a Word Processor.

How can I return to ASCII?

A: SAS uses a special ANSI character set for box borders and other special features in the Output Window. You have to change the characters used for boxes and other features as follows:

```
OPTIONS  FORMCHAR='|----|+|---+=|-/\<>*';
```

NOTE that the string after FORMCHAR= needs to be enclosed in single quotes (as shown) and needs to be exactly the characters shown in the example, in the same order.

The '|' character is the vertical bar, usually located on the same key as the backslash.

Question 75: Truncation of SAS numeric values

SAS has a TRUNC function that truncates specified numbers but does not allow the use of variable names as arguments. SAS has a ROUND function that ROUNDS numbers, but does not do true truncation when the rounded-off part is greater than 5.

SAS has an INT function that truncates to the integer before a decimal point.

How can I truncate a number to two decimal points?

A: The only way to get your two-decimal true truncation is to multiply by 100, then use INT then divide by 100 as follows:

Since you apparently cannot specify decimal places for 'truncation':

```
data temp; input a;

cards;

5.897452

;

data temp2; set temp; drop a b c;

b=a*100; c=int(b); d=c/100;

run;
```

Question 76: Redirecting SAS Log and Output

How ca I log and output information to appear in the same file so that my program statements will be followed by their output for comparison of SAS statements and the output they generate?

A: Use PROC PRINTTO with two FILENAME statements, but make both FILENAME statements point to the same file.

EXAMPLE:

```
options linesize=80;

/* TWO diferent filename statements point to the same
'output' file   */

filename test1 'file1.out';
filename test2 'file1.out';

/* PROC PRINTTO redirects the log (LOG) and output
(PRINT) files    */

proc printto log=test1 print=test2;
data temp; input a b;
cards;

4 5

5 4

3 3

6 8

4 6

5 6
;

proc glm; model a=b;
proc corr;
proc freq;

run;
```

Question 77: Using SPSS Data (Portable File) in SAS

How do I convert an SPSS Portable file to an SAS Data Set?

A: SAS can read data originally saved in SPSS if it is in the form of an SPSS Export file. SPSS Export files are created in SPSS with the EXPORT OUTFILE=<filename>. command, or by clicking File>Save As and creating a *.por (portable) file.

If they are created in another system, they are moved (*not* in binary mode) to the system where SAS will be converting them.

Note that the issue of converting SPSS Value Label information into SAS is a separate topic covered in detail below. If you have no Value Labels in SPSS, or are willing to 'do without' them in your SAS data set, you may ignore that section.

In UNIX:

This example shows the statements needed to read an SPSS Export file and output an SAS Data Set in UNIX:

`libname test '~/sasdata';` * This is where the SAS Data Set will be written;

`libname apple spss 'spss.por';` * This names your SPSS Export file and uses the SPSS read engine;

`proc copy in=apple out=test;`

`run;`

`proc print data=test._first_ ;` * This is to see if it works;

`run;`

You may want to rename the SAS Data Set (_first_ is somewhat awkward). This can be done with an operating system command (in UNIX, the command is "mv") or in SAS.

To rename it in SAS, run the following statements:

```
proc datasets library=test;

change _first_=avocado;
run;
```

In Windows or Macintosh:

To use the above example in other operating systems, the two LIBNAME statements must be changed to point to directories and/or files appropriate for the operating system; otherwise, the rest of the statements shown above are exactly the same under SAS for Windows or Macintosh.

SAS for Windows (or SAS-PC) LIBNAME statements:

`libname test 'c:\sasdata';` * This is where the SAS Data Set will be written;

`libname apple spss 'c:\spss.export';` * This names your SPSS Export file and uses the SPSS read engine;

SAS for Macintosh LIBNAME statements:

`libname test 'Hard_Disk:MySASFiles:';` * This is where the SAS Data Set will be written;

`libname apple spss 'Hard_Disk:Desktop:spss.export';` * This names your SPSS Export file and uses the SPSS read engine;

Converting SPSS Value Labels into SAS User-Defined Formats:

There is no method provided by either SAS or SPSS to convert SPSS Value Labels into SAS Formats.

Many difficult issues are involved, but the problems mostly stem from the following basic difference:

SPSS Value Labels are stored along with the data in the SPSS Active File (or, in permanent form, in the SPSS Save File);

SAS labels for individual values are called Formats, and are stored in a Format Library which is an SAS Catalog separate from the SAS data set.

UCS provides a program to perform this conversion. It is called spss2sas.prg.

It may be downloaded from this link by clicking on the filename, or it may be found in almaak at

~gpjones/users/spss2sas.prg,

or in aludra at

~jerryj/users/spss2sas.prg.

The program will work in SAS for Windows or SAS for Macintosh. Once downloaded, you can run the program as shown in the instructions below.

The program will display some windows in which you can specify the information necessary for SAS to convert the SPSS Value Label information into SAS Formats. Before running the SAS program, of course, you must prepare the SPSS Data file to be processed by SAS.

Here are the instructions for converting SPSS Data and Value Labels into an SAS Data Set with SAS Formats:

1. The best thing to do first is to choose a name for the set of files that the program will use and create. The name should be 8 characters or less, and must begin with a character.

    Let's say you choose 'my1st' as the name. You should use that name when you create the two SPSS files used as input (described below):

    ```
    my1st.por    my1st.txt
    ```

    And you should use the same name when prompted within the program's windows for the SAS data set (which would become my1st.sas7bdat) and the prefix for the two format-name files that the program creates:

```
my1st.prc    my1st.fmt
```

When choosing a name, keep in mind that it should be meaningful -- related to the nature of the data or project with which the files are associated -- and it must be unique, so as not to overwrite or conflict with other files in the directories you use to store files.

The example 'my1st' will be used in these instructions.

2. Create a text file with the SPSS Value Label information in it. Each version of SPSS gives you the ability to display and save the Dictionary information for your SPSS data. The spss2sas program uses this information to create the SAS Formats later.

    Once the data are read into an SPSS Active File, you can display and save the Dictionary information, which includes the Value Labels. In the Windows and Macintosh versions, the Active File will appear as data in the spreadsheet-like Data Window.

    Before creating the text file as described here, it is important that you DELETE everything from the Output window just before running the DISPLAY command, or just before clicking the File Info button.
    This instruction will be repeated below.

    In SPSS for Windows or Macintosh: With the Active File in place (i.e., the data are visible in the Data Window), and the Output Window either deleted or cleared (to remove any previous output), open a Syntax window and enter and run the following:

    ```
    DISPLAY DICTIONARY.
    EXECUTE.
    ```

    Click File > Export, then choose the *.txt file type, then enter a path and file name (e.g., c:\sastuff\my1st.txt) and click OK.

3. Save the Active File into a Portable (*.por) file. In the Windows or Macintosh versions, with the Data Window (Active File) active, click File>Save As, then choose the *.por

file type, enter a file name (e.g., my1st.por) then click OK. If
you prefer to use a Syntax window, enter and run the
following:

```
EXPORT  OUTFILE='my1st.por'.

EXECUTE.
```

4. Now that you have created the SPSS files needed for input,
    you are ready to run the SAS program that does the
    conversion.

    If you prefer, you can find a copy in almaak (RCF) or aludra
    (SCF).

    After the last window appears and you exit the program, you
    will have a file called spss2sas.prg.log, which will contain a
    record of the conversion program's work. If there were
    problems, they will be noted in this LOG file.

    NOTE: When PROC COPY reads an SPSS Portable (*.por)
    file that is bad, there is no information to this effect in the
    Log. It looks like everything went OK. If you see a later error
    message to the effect that CONVERT._FIRST_ was not
    found, you should suspect that the SPSS Portable file is bad,
    and re-create it,
    ideally on the same system where the SAS program is
    running.

5. The conversion program creates an SAS data set, stored in
    any directory you specify. In addition, the program creates
    two files that are used during the program's execution and
    are then saved in the directory you specify, in case you need
    them in the future.
    a. my1st.prc -- this is the PROC FORMAT statement
        that creates all the formats necessary to
        accommodate what were the SPSS value labels.
        Formats are named consecutively and begin with the
        prefix letter(s) you specify while the conversion
        program is running.

        For example, if you specify 'ab' as the format prefix,
        the program creates AB1FMT., AB2FMT., AB3FMT.,
        and so forth, until all needed formats are created. If

you chose 'temporary'when the program asked you about how to store the formats, then this PROC FORMAT statement stored in 'my1st.prc' will need to be run each time you use the SAS data set created by the conversion program. If you chose 'permanent' there is no need to run this PROC FORMAT each time (though it will be necessary for the formats.scto1 or formats.sc2 file that holds the permanent formats to be made available to SAS whenever the SAS data set is accessed.

   b.   my1st.fmt -- This is the FORMAT statement that is used when the SAS data set is being created by the conversion program. Normally, you will not need to use this FORMAT statement as such in the future, but it could be useful as a 'map' to which formats are being used for which variables. Since the format names themselves have to be arbitrary (e.g.supra, AB1FMT., AB2FMT., etc.), this will be the most convenient way to match variables and their format names.

6.   Here are some examples of how to use the SAS Data Set and Formats created with the conversion program. The examples assume that you have stored all files in a subdirectory called c:\sasstuff or HardDisk:SasStuff, depending on the operating system. These examples will use the first (i.e., Windows) syntax. If your operating system is a Macintosh, substitute accordingly.

If you chose 'permanent' formats:

```
--------------------------------
libname library 'c:\sasstuff';
libname storesas 'c:\sasstuff';

proc print data=storesas.my1st;

run;
```

The LIBRARY libref is necessary to point SAS to the permanent formats catalog.

If you chose 'temporary' formats:

```
libname storesas 'c:\sasstuff';

%include 'c:\sasstuff/my1st.prc';
proc print data-storesas.my1st;
run;
```

The %INCLUDE statement calls in the PROC FORMAT stored in my1st.prc. If you prefer, you can use other methods to run the PROC FORMAT statement found in my1st.prc. For example, you can copy my1st.prc into another file, such as now.sas, then add the LIBNAME and DATA or PROC steps of your choice, then run the now.sas program as a unit. It might look like:

```
proc format;

value ablfmt. <etc., as found in my1st.prc>

. . .

libname storesas 'c:\sasstuff';
data subset1; set storesas.my1st;
keep <variable list>;
proc freq; tables <variable list>;

run;
```

Question 78: Using SAS Data (Transport File) in SPSS

How can I get SPSS to use data originally saved in SAS?

A: As of Version 10.1, SPSS can now read SAS data sets directly, whereas before this version an SAS Transport File was necessary. Here is a summary of some of the current techniques.

SPSS Version 10.1 and above:

SAS data sets (Version 7 of SAS and above) are stored in files with a *.sas7bdat extension. These files can now be read directly into the SPSS Data Window.

Click File>Open>Data, then choose 'SAS Long File Name' (or other choice appropriate for your SAS data set), then locate the folder and file you want to convert so that the name of that file appears in the 'File Name' field, then click 'Open'.

SAS Transport Files can also be converted into the SPSS Data Window (Active File) in Version 10.1 and above.

SPSS Version 10.0.x and lower:

Older versions of SPSS traditionally required any data from SAS to be in the form of a Version 5 SAS Transport File, which is the type created by using a LIBNAME statement with the XPORT engine (not one created using PROC CPORT). This, of course, limited users to data that conformed to the old (pre-Version 7) SAS rules, with variable names of eight characters or less, and so forth.

This type of conversion is available on all platforms running SPSS version 5 or higher.

The following is a very basic example of how to create an SAS transport file using the XPORT engine. (The example assumes you have a temporary SAS data set called "MYDATA5".)

```
LIBNAME OUT1 XPORT 'sasfile.xpt';
```

```
PROC   COPY   IN=WORK   OUT=OUT1;   SELECT   MYDATA5;

RUN;
```

Remember that SAS transport files must be moved from system to system in BINARY mode, so if the SAS transport file was created elsewhere, move it to UNIX in BINARY.

To read in the SAS transport file created in the example above, and save it as an SPSS system (Save) file, use the following commands in SPSS session:

```
get sas data='sasfile.xpt' dset(mydata5).
save outfile='newdata.sps'.
execute.
```

This operation also can be done using the File>Open>Data menu choices in later versions.

The sub command DSET(MYDATA5) is not necessary, unless the transport file contains more than one SAS data set.
Converting SAS Formats into SPSS Value Labels

SAS allows users to write their own format specifications to assign labels to values. (SPSS calls these 'value labels', and stores them along with data; SAS calls them 'formats', and stores them separately.) If your SAS data set has imbedded user-written format specifications, you can usually convert these types of formats into SPSS value labels by adding the FORMATS sub command to the GET SAS command.

First, the formats must be converted to an SAS transport file, in a process analogous to the one outlined above for SAS data sets. First, the formats must be put into an SAS data set using PROC FORMAT with the CNTLOUT= option, as in this example:

```
LIBNAME SASDATA 'C:\SASDATA';**(or '~/sasdata' ***;

LIBNAME LIBRARY 'C:\SASFMTS';**(or '~/sasfmts' ***;

PROC FORMAT LIBRARY=LIBRARY CNTLOUT=SASDATA.FMTXPORT;

RUN;
```

NOTE: It is advisable NOT to use the name FORMATS as in SASDATA.FORMATS when using the CNTLOUT= option of PROC FORMAT. This is to avoid confusion with the SAS format catalog, which is called FORMATS.SCT01.

Next, create another SAS transport file as you did for the data:

```
LIBNAME OUT2 XPORT 'sasfmts.xpt;'

PROC COPY IN=SASDATA OUT=OUT2; SELECT FMTXPORT;

RUN;
```

Then, your SPSS program would look like this:

```
get sas data='sasfile.xpt' dset(mydata5)

/ formats='sasfmts.xpt'.

save outfile='newdata.sps'.

execute.
```

Question 79: Converting Access, Excel, and dBase-type files into SAS Data Sets

How can I enter a data in Excel, dBase, or Lotus format by using a data in SAS without writing out Raw (ASCII) data or re-entering?

A: SAS for Windows and SAS for Macintosh can read .XLS, .DBF and .DIF files easily.

If you want to use your data base data in UNIX, you need to do a couple of extra steps, outlined at the end of this document, namely, convert your SAS data set into a transport file, upload it (in Binary mode, always) to UNIX, then convert it back into an SAS data set there.

CONVERTING dBASE, LOTUS and EXCEL-type DATA INTO AN SAS DATA SET (and vice versa)

SAS provides three basic ways to convert data base files from other types of software into SAS Data Sets, and vice versa. The more difficult, but more flexible method is to use SAS/ACCESS software, either from ACCESS Windows or with PROC ACCESS syntax.

(In order to use this method, SAS/ACCESS software must be installed. SAS/ACCESS is provided with SAS/BASE when distributed by UCS, but must be installed as a separate add-on by the user.)

An easier method, if you have (or can make) .DBF or .DIF files, is to use PROC DBF or PROC DIF.
The easiest method (if you have SAS for Windows 6.12) is the "Import Wizard".

These three methods are outlined below. Note that PROC DBF and PROC DIF are available for Windows and Macintosh only in Release 6.10 and later (and, of course, in SAS-PC, Release 6.04).

.XLS and other types of files -- the "Import Wizard"

SAS for Windows and SAS for the Macintosh as of Release 6.12 have an "Import Wizard" that allows you to point-and-click your way through a simple process that imports .XLS, .DBF, .WK1, .WK3, and .WK4 files, as well as files with data delimited by commas and other characters.

Click on File > Import Data and follow the instructions, if you have one of these types of files.

To write out an SAS Data Set to an Excel File format, click File > Export Data to create the Excel version;

NOTE 1 -- SAS 6.x only knows older versions of Excel: If you are saving your data from Excel into an .xls file for use in SAS Version 6.x, you must use the option that specifies 'Excel 5.0/7.0' or 'Excel 5.0/95', or even an earlier version such as 'Excel 4.0' (not the more recent types of .xls files available in versions such as Excel 97). Otherwise, SAS may fail to import the file, giving an OLE2 error.

NOTE 2 -- Number fields may get lost in SAS data sets unless converted: Numeric fields in Excel sometimes do not translate correctly to SAS unless they are "declared" as Text in Excel before the conversion is made. It is not sufficient to use Format Cells>Number (or Text) to make this conversion.

Click Data>Text-to-Columns>Choose Delimiter (Tab is usually correct) then click the Text radio button to make the conversion. After the file is saved, you can then use the SAS Import Wizard (or PROC IMPORT) to bring the data into SAS.

NOTE 3 -- Excel Workbooks with multiple Worksheets: When you want to import multiple Worksheets (or a Worksheet other than Sheet1) from an Excel Workbook, you can specify the Worksheet you want using the "Options" button that activates when you choose (or specify) the .xls file you are trying to import.

Note that the field which appears after clicking "Options" (labeled "Worksheet/Range" in Version 7 and higher) may be empty. You can see a list of available Worksheets by clicking the down-arrow at the right of the field.

.DBF and some .DIF files:

SAS for Windows and SAS for the Macintosh can read .DBF file formats and some types of .DIF formats. .DBF is a format used in dBase and other software, and .DIF is a format used in Lotus and elsewhere.

Note that not all .DIF formats are constructed the same. SAS seems to be able to convert the older Lotus-made .DIF files, but not the newer types created by Microsoft Access and Excel. When in doubt, try a .DBF format or, if you have the necessary Release level of SAS, try the file types that the "Import Wizard".

When outputting a .DIF file from an SAS data set for use in spreadsheet (or other) software, it seems there are no problems like those found when trying to input .DIF to SAS. .DIF files created by SAS normally can be read in old Lotus or in new Microsoft Access and Excel versions.

PROC DBF and PROC DIF:

To convert a dBase file to an SAS Data Set, run PROC DBF as in this example. We assume here that we have a dBase V file called tommy.dbf in the current directory, and the SAS data set called tomsas will be temporary.

```
filename tom 'tommy.dbf';

proc dbf db5=tom out=tomsas;

run;
```

To convert an SAS Data Set into a dBase file, run PROC DBF as in the following example. We assume here that we have a permanent SAS Data Set called "medical" in a directory called "C:\mysas", and that we want to create a dBase IV file called "medicine.dbf" to be stored on the diskette in the A: drive.

```
libname oldsas 'c:\mysas';
filename newdbf 'a:\medicine.dbf';

proc dbf db4=newdbf data=oldsas.medical;

run;
```

To convert a .DIF file to an SAS Data Set, run PROC DIF as in this example. We assume here that we have a .DIF file called "thomas.dif" in the current directory, and the SAS data set called "thomasas" will be temporary.

```
filename thom 'thomas.dif';

proc dif dif=thom out=thomasas;

run;
```

To convert an SAS Data Set into a .DIF file, run PROC DIF as in the following example. We assume here that we have a permanent SAS Data Set called "medinfo" in a directory called "C:\mysas", and that we want to create a .DIF file called "medinfo.dif" to be stored on the diskette in the A: drive.

```
libname oldsas 'c:\mysas';

filename newdif 'a:\medinfo.dif';

proc dif dif=newdif data=oldsas.medinfo;

run;
```

As you can see, PROC DIF works in the same way as the examples shown above for PROC DBF, although there are more choices you may need to make, including whether you want to specify a variable name prefix (the default is COLn, where "n" is the ordinal number in which the variable appears: COL1, COL2, etc.), whether you want to skip a row or rows at the beginning of the .DIF file, etc.

Note that these examples use DOS file specifications. The same SAS statements will work in SAS for the Macintosh with Mac file specifications in place of the DOS examples.

SAS/ACCESS Interface to PC File Formats:

If you prefer to customize your SAS Data Set and read in only certain variables from the .DBF or .DIF file, or change variable names or formats.

For example, you can use SAS/ACCESS software. SAS/ACCESS also can read .XLS and other file types. This is done by invoking ACCESS and by making choices and filling in fields in a series of SAS/ACCESS windows.

Following is an outline (with notations) of a typical SAS/ACCESS session in which a .DBF file is converted into an SAS Data Set. The procedure for converting .DIF files is similar. In any case, this is just an overview, and only the very brave should attempt these operations without a manual.

To understand the process of converting a .DBF or .DIF file to an SAS Data Set (or an SAS View, if you wish), you should notice first that there are three major steps:

• Point SAS to the relevant input and output files.

• Create an Access Descriptor to 'map' the .DBF or .DIF file.

• Create a View Descriptor to describe the new SAS Data Set (or SAS View).

Here is a typical scenario for creating a customized SAS Data Set from an existing .DBF file:

If you wish to store the new SAS Data Set permanently, issue a LIBNAME statement to tell SAS where you want it stored:

```
LIBNAME XYZSAS 'C:\';
```

Start SAS/ACCESS either by clicking on Globals>Access>Access Database Files, or by running the following program:

```
PROC ACCESS;

RUN;
```

The Access Window will appear, showing all SAS Data Sets available to your system at that moment:

Click File>New to create a new Access Descriptor

You will see the "New" window in which you enter the LIBREF for the directory where you want the Access Descriptor to be stored and the NAME you want it to have. An Access Descriptor is an SAS File that can be re-used in the future. Example:

LIBREF   NAME   TYPE
Access Name: XYZSAS . DBFTEST1 . ACCESS

Click OK.

Next you go to the Select Data Window, where you highlight
".DBF Files" and click OK.

Next is the ACCESS: Create Descriptor Window, where you must
fill in the path to where the .DBF file is stored. This specification
is really the path and the first part of the .dbf file name, not
including the .dbf extension. Let's say your file is
"C:\DBASE\TOCONVRT.DBF". In this window, you should see:

Path: C:\DBASE\TOCONVRT

Next the list of variables found in the .DBF file is displayed. Here
you can choose which variables you want to delete from the .DBF
file (type 'D' in the 'Func' filed on the line where each variable is
listed). You can also type new variable names under "SAS
Names", if you want to change the original .DBF names. When
you are finished modifying this window, click Locals>End.

Next, you are returned to the ACCESS: Create Descriptor
Window, where you should click File>End to ask SAS to save the
Descriptor and continue.

Now, in the main ACCESS Window, find the Access Descriptor
you have just created and saved. It will be listed as
___XYZSAS   DBFTEST1   ACCESS

Type "CV" (Create View) on the line to the left of the name. This
will bring up the View Descriptor Display Window, in which you
specify both the name for the View Descriptor, and the name for
the output SAS Data Set. Your window might look like this:

Descriptor: Library: OLD   Member: DBFVIEW1 Type:
VIEW

Output SAS Data Set: Library: OLD   Member: DBF2SAS

Path: C:\DBASE\TOCONVRT.DBF

<variable listing, with Action fields, etc.>

When you have finished customizing this view (note that unlike
the Access Descriptor where you deselect variables if you wish,

no variables are selected here unless you type 'S' under 'Func'), click Locals>End, and you will return to the main ACCESS Window, and both your View Descriptor and your final SAS Data Set will be written (as shown in the SAS Log).

MOVING AN SAS DATA SET FROM WINDOWS OR MACINTOSH TO UNIX:

PROC IMPORT (and the Import Wizard) on the UNIX platform currently can process only dBase (*.dbf) files, so file formats other than *.dbf created in Windows must be changed to *.dbf files before attempting to import them to SAS on the UNIX platform. This is explained in detail in the SAS document stored here (please click).

Another method (perhaps more dependable and predictable) for moving data in special PC file formats to SAS under UNIX is to import them into SAS for Windows first (using PROC IMPORT or the Import Wizard, as noted above), then create an SAS Transport File using PROC CPORT, then transmit the file (in BINARY mode only) to UNIX, then unravel the transport file there using PROC CIMPORT.

To move an SAS data set between unlike systems, such as from a Windows machine to UNIX, you need to make an SAS Transport File out of the SAS Data Set that you wish to move.

If you have converted an Excel .xls file into an SAS data set called "project4" which is now stored in a subdirectory under Windows ("C:\SASDATA"). (Of course, the procedures shown below will work on any SAS data set, not just those that used to be Excel data.) Here is a scenario for moving the data to UNIX.

Under Windows or Macintosh:

Run PROC CPORT to make a transport file. (Example uses Windows file references.)

```
libname mydat 'c:\sasdata';

filename trans1 'c:\tmp\datamove.xpo';
proc cport data=mydat.project4 file=trans1
sortinfo=no;
run;
```

The PROC CPORT statement reads the SAS data set and writes the transport file into the DOS file referenced by TRANS1, namely "datamove.xpo".

NOTE: Once SAS for UNIX is upgraded to match the current version of SAS for Windows, the SORTINFO=NO option of PROC CPORT will no longer be necessary. See the entry in this FAQ directory called "Making Transport Files in SAS for Windows..." for more information. Also, if using SAS for the Macintosh, the SORTINFO=NO option should be omitted.

Moving the File:

Use WS-FTP, Kermit, or any other file transfer protocol (consult the documentation for your communication software; if you're in a user room, use WS-FTP on Windows and Fetch on a Macintosh), and move the file *in BINARY mode* (this is essential) to your UNIX account.

For this example, we'll put it in a UNIX subdirectory of your home directory, called "~/fromthepc".

Under UNIX:

Once the file is moved to UNIX into a subdirectory called "~/fromthepc" (this is an arbitrary example; it can be stored anywhere), run the following program to convert the transport file back into an SAS data set and store it in your home directory (again, an arbitrary choice; you can store your SAS data sets anywhere you want).

```
libname storeit '~/';

filename datain '~/fromthepc';

proc cimport library=storeit infile=datain;

run;
```

SAS will re-create the original SAS data set with its original name (which in our example is called PROJECT4), ready for your use in any UNIX SAS session.

Question 80: Dealing with Date Values from Excel or Access Databases

When I convert data from Excel, Access, or other database software, the date values are not the same as SAS date values, so when calculations are done, the resulting numbers are much larger than expected.

A: When SAS reads date values from database software such as Excel or Access, it has to assume that the values are actually date/time values, not only a number of days, but hours, minutes and seconds as well. The "usual" SAS date value represents the number of days after (or before) 01 January 1960. SAS date time values, such as those resulting from date values in Excel and Access, represent the number of seconds after (or before) 01 January 1960, and these, obviously, are much larger numbers.

You can convert these values in different ways, depending on how you want to use them. You can extract the DATE portion of a DATETIME value, then use the result as you would any SAS DATE value, or you can do your calculations with the original values then compensate by dividing by the necessary day, month, or year values.

For example, you want to know the number of years between two date points. Our original Excel or Access database contains a Date of Birth (DOB) variable and a Date of Visit (VISIT) variable, and we want to know how old each person was at the time of VISIT. Let's use ACCDATA as our data set name in the example:

ACCDATA (as it appears formatted using PROC PRINT):

```
ID        DOB                 VISIT

1    09MAY1951:00:00:00   03JUN2000:00:00:00

2    29FEB1976:00:00:00   12APR2001:00:00:00

3    31OCT1938:00:00:00   30SEP2001:00:00:00

4    12AUG1925:00:00:00   28JAN2000:00:00:00
```

```
5    01JAN1964:00:00:00    24DEC2001:00:00:00
```

Another solution is to convert the DOB and VISIT DATETIME variables into DATE variables, then calculate your AGE variable by dividing the result by 365.25 (the average number of days in a year, correcting for Leap Year).

This can be done with the DATEPART function. The formats are optional, but helpful in viewing the output.

```
data agecalc1; set accdata;

format dob visit datetime18.

dobnew visitnew mmddyy8.;
dobnew=datepart(dob);

visitnew=datepart(visit);

age = (visitnew - dobnew) / 365.25;

proc print;

run;
```

The resulting data, shown by PROC PRINT, looks like:

```
ID     DOB                  VISIT          DOBNEW  VISITNEW
AGE


1  09MAY51:00:00:00  03JUN00:00:00:00  05/09/51
06/03/00     9.0705


2  29FEB76:00:00:00  12APR01:00:00:00  02/29/76
04/12/01    25.1170


3  31OCT38:00:00:00  30SEP01:00:00:00  10/31/38
09/30/01    62.9158


4  12AUG25:00:00:00  28JAN00:00:00:00  08/12/25
01/28/00    74.4613
```

5 01JAN64:00:00:00   24DEC01:00:00:00   01/01/64
12/24/01   37.9795

And the last solution is to calculate the AGE variable from the original DOB and VISIT variables (in DATETIME format), and divide by the number of seconds in a year, which is

60*60*24*365.25 = 31557600

Here's the example, and the output:

```
data agecalc1; set accdata;

format dob visit datetime18.

age = (visit - dob) / 31557600;

proc print;
run;
```

ID	DOB	VISIT	AGE
1	09MAY51:00:00:00	03JUN00:00:00:00	9.0705
2	29FEB76:00:00:00	12APR01:00:00:00	25.1170
3	31OCT38:00:00:00	30SEP01:00:00:00	62.9158
4	12AUG25:00:00:00	28JAN00:00:00:00	74.4613
5	01JAN64:00:00:00	24DEC01:00:00:00	37.9795

Question 81: Lost Variables (Columns) when Importing Data from Other Software

Some versions of dBase, Excel and other software have a built-in limitation of the number of variables that can be moved from those packages into SPSS or SAS. One known dBase limit is 255 variables, but this number may vary from software to software, or even from version to version in a particular software package. This is not an SPSS or SAS problem, but a problem with the software that originally created the data file.

The symptoms of this problem include the fact that some variables (columns) get imported into SPSS or SAS correctly, and the data look fine, but not all variables make the transition. This has been noticed with .DBF type files, but may occur with other types as well. In general, this problem is less and less frequent as the other software packages become more sophisticated.

A: The solution to this problem that is most often recommended is to split the data file into less-than-255 variable portions, making sure to assign an unique id-number variable to each of the split portions, then move the data into SPSS or SAS, and then merge the portions back together.

Question 82: Preserving Formatted Values When Moving SAS Data to Spreadsheet Software

I have some data in SAS that uses formats that I have written, and I want to move the data to Excel (or Access, or dBase, or any other software for which SAS can export data), but I want the values to be the formatted values, not the original data values.

EXAMPLE: PROC PRINT (without formatting) shows the following values:

SEX	SCORE1	SCORE2
1	42	51
2	65	23
1	43	27

But when I use the variable SEX, I always ask SAS to employ the user-written format (sexfmt.) where 1='female' and 2='male', as follows:

SEX	SCORE1	SCORE2
female	42	51
male	65	23
female	43	27

A: SAS allows the creation of a new variable in which the formats become the actual data. This is done with an assignment statement in which the PUT function is used:

```
NEWVAR=PUT(OLDVAR,FORMAT.);
```

All values that match the specifications in the format (i.e., all values that are either 1 ["female"] or 2 ["male"]) will have the words stored instead of the original numbers. All other values missing data coded as 9, for example, or mis-coded values will remain the same, as there is no substitution specified for them in the format.

Sample program to illustrate making a new variable that store formatted values (rather than original values);

```
/** the format is created and stored (in the temporary library)
**/

proc format;
value sexfmt 1='female'

2='male';
```

/** the data are read in as numeric values (PROC PRINT with a FORMAT statement is used to illustrate the difference between this and the final step) **/

```
data temp; input sex score1 score2;
cards;
1       42      51

2       65      23

1       43      27
;

proc print;

format sex sexfmt.;

run;
```

/** the new variable (GENDER) is created to store the formatted values as actual data, and PROC PRINT (with no FORMAT statement) is used to illustrate this new version of the data; notice that the variable SEX holds the original numeric values, while GENDER is a character variable with the formatted values (the words FEMALE and MALE) as actual data; when moved to other software such as dBase, Access, Excel and so forth, the data values for GENDER will be 'female' and 'male' (not 1 and 2)
*/

```
data temp2; set temp;

gender=put(sex,sexfmt.);
```

```
proc print data=temp2;

run;
```

```
/************************************************************
/
```
*** Sample program to illustrate possible shortcuts when many variables are involved; MANY

/*** If many variables have formats assigned to them, it may be possible to use some handy SAS shortcuts to save programming time and space. This technique uses the ARRAY language, and will work if a number of variables use the same format. (Different variables using different formats will still have to be recorded separately, as shown above). ***/

EXAMPLE: PROC PRINT (without formatting) shows the following values:

```
ID    ITEM1    ITEM2    ITEM3    ITEM4    ITEM5

1     1        2        1        1        1
2     2        2        2        9        1
3     2        9        1        1        2
```

The ITEM in variables is question on a survey which ask for a 'yes' or 'no' answer and they are coded originally as 1s and 2s. A format called yesno is used to allow SAS to display the words instead of the numbers, if requested. PROC PRINT with a FORMAT statement makes the output look like:

```
ID    ITEM1    ITEM2    ITEM3    ITEM4    ITEM5

1     yes      no       yes      yes      yes
2     no       no       no       9        yes
3     no       9        yes      yes      no
```

Notice that the 9s, which represent missing values, will stay the same since the format in this example (see below) doesn't assign any new value to numbers other than 1s and 2s.

/** the format is created and stored (in the temporary library) **/

```
proc format;
value yesno 1='yes'

2='no';
```

/** the data are read in as numeric values (PROC PRINT with a
FORMAT statement is used to illustrate the difference between
this and the final step)**/

```
data temp; input id item1-item5;
cards;
1  1  2  1  1  1

2  2  2  2  9  1

3  2  9  1  1  2

;
proc print;

format item1-item5 yesno.;

run;
```

/** the new variables (NEWITEMn) are created to store the
formatted values as actual data, and PROC
PRINT (with no FORMAT statement) is used to illustrate this
new version of the data; notice that the variables ITEMn hold the
original numeric values, while NEWITEMn are character
variables with the formatted values (the words YES and NO) as
actual data;

When moved to other software such as dBase, Access, Excel and
so forth, the data values for NEWITEMn will be 'yes' and 'no'
(not 1 and 2) */

```
data temp2; set temp; drop I;

array oldies{5} item1-item5;

array newbies{5} $ newitem1-newitem5;

do i=1 to 5;
newbies{i}=put(oldies{i},yesno.);

end;
```

```
proc print data=temp2;
run;
```

Question 83: SAS Transport Files

How can I make transport file using PROC CPORT?

And how do I unravel it again into a true SAS Date Set?

A: There is one basic procedure to perform these tasks. However, because there are numerous different platforms that SAS operates under, small differences do arise every now and then. What follows are two examples of the same procedure on each of two different platforms, UNIX and Windows, for Version 5 and Version 6 and higher.

Version 5

Note 1: This PROC COPY method of making a transport file should be used only when necessary. PROC CPORT should be used if possible.

The following situations are examples of when PROC COPY must be used:

1. When re-converting a transport file originally made with PROC COPY.

2. When transporting a Version 5 SAS Data Set.

3. When transporting a file from a Release higher than 6.06 down to a lower release.

NOTE 2: SAS transport files must be sent in binary mode. When moving files using ftp, make sure the 'binary' choice is checked (usually a radio button or check-box) before transferring the file. If using command-line ftp, issue the command 'binary' before sending.

UNIX
----

1. Creating a PROC COPY transport file.

    ```
    options replace;  * Needed for 6.09 under UNIX;
    ```

    ```
    libname olddata '~/username';  * This is where the SAS
    ```
    data sets are;

    ```
    libname plum  xport '~/sending.dta';  * This is what
    ```
    the transport file is called;

    ```
    proc copy in=olddata out=plum;
    ```

    ```
    select orange grape;
    ```

2. Unraveling a PROC COPY transport file.

    ```
    libname olddata '~/sasdata';  * SAS Data Sets will be
    ```
    written here;

    ```
    libname pear xport '~/incoming.data';  * This is what
    ```
    the transport file is called;

    ```
    proc copy in=pear out=olddata;
    ```

    ```
    select peach guava;
    ```


Windows
----

1. Creating a transport file

    ```
    libname olddata 'c:\sasdata';  * This is the location of
    ```
    the SAS data sets;

    ```
    libname  plum  xport  'a:sending.dta';  * This is what
    ```
    the transport file is called;

    ```
    proc copy in=olddata out=plum;
    ```

    ```
    select orange grape;
    ```

2. Unraveling a transport file

```
libname olddata 'c:\sasdata'; * New SAS Data Sets
will be written here;

libname pear sasv5xpt 'a:incoming.dta'; * This is
what the transport file is called;

proc copy in=pear out=olddata;

select peach guava;
```

Version 6 and higher

NOTE 1: This PROC CPORT method of making and unraveling transport files should be used whenever possible. It cannot be used if transporting from Release 6.06 and above down to a lower release. It also cannot be used when dealing with a Version 5 SAS Data Set or any SAS transport file that was created using PROC COPY.

NOTE 2: SAS transport files must be sent in binary mode. When moving files using ftp, make sure the 'binary' choice is checked (usually a radio button or check-box) before transferring the file. If using command-line ftp, issue the command 'binary' before sending.

UNIX
----

1. Sending from UNIX to another system

```
libname olddata '~/sasdata'; * This is where the
SAS Data Set(s) reside;

filename guava '~/sending.dat'; * This names the
transport file 'sending.dat';

proc cport data=olddata.mydata1 file=guava;
```

2. Reconverting on UNIX (file sent in from another system)

```
libname olddata '~/sasdata'; * SAS Data Sets will
be written here;

filename cumquat '~/incoming.dat'; * This tells
SAS the name of the transport file;

proc cimport library=olddata infile=cumquat;
```

NOTE: If you are using PROC CPORT/PROC CIMPORT to move files from one version of SAS to another on the same operating system.

For example, from Version 8 of SAS under UNIX to Version 9 of SAS under UNIX (as a substitute for PROC MIGRATE, which doesn't always work properly), you must use two different subdirectories, or "libraries" as SAS calls them, one for the original files (LIBRARY= in the PROC CPORT statement) and a different one for the new files (LIBRARY= in the PROC CIMPORT statement).

Windows
----
1. Sending from SAS for Windows to another system

```
libname olddata 'c:\sasdata'; * This is where the
SAS Data Set(s) reside;

filename guava 'a:sending.dat'; * This names the
transport file 'sending.dat';

proc cport data=olddata.mydata1 file=guava;
```

2. Reconverting on SAS for Windows (file sent in from another system)

```
libname olddata 'c:\sasdata'; * SAS Data Sets
will be written here;

filename cumquat 'a:\sending.dat'; * This tells
SAS the name of the transport file;

proc cimport library=olddata infile=cumquat;
```

Question 84: Converting Old SAS FSEDIT Screens and other SAS Catalogs to Version 8.x

I have an old SAS Catalog originally created in 6.04 (SAS-PC).

How can I use it in Version 8?

A: If the file has been converted already to 6.08 or higher, the following steps will allow you to further convert it to Version 8.x (If the file has not yet been converted to 6.08 or higher, this conversion can only be done in Release 6.04, and may have to be done by SAS Institute people [for a fee, of course] or, in a few cases, by ITS staff.

In Version 6.12 of SAS:

1. Open your screen and full data set in 6.12;

2. Type MOD (followed by password, if there is one) on the command line;

3. Choose '3' from the menu, this opens the original SCL code;

4. Type END on the command line, this recompiles the code, and you should get a message in the lower left that the compile was successful;

5. Run PROC CPORT in 6.12 to make an export file containing the data and screen;

6. Run PROC CIMPORT in 8.1 to 'import' the data and screen, store the data and screen in a different directory from that containing the Version 6 files converted in Step 5. The data and screen now should be usable in Version 8.

Question 85: Using a Macintosh SAS Program File in SAS for Windows

The SAS program that I saved in a Macintosh SAS session doesn't format properly when I try to use it in SAS for Windows. Specifically, all the program statements are on a single line, with 'funny characters' [empty squares, for example] at the point where each line should end.

A: Files saved from an SAS window (such as the Program Editor) are ASCII files. In the Macintosh, each line is terminated with a Carriage Return (ASCII 13). ASCII files in DOS however need both a Line Feed and a Carriage Return (ASCII 13 and 10).

When files come to DOS with only a Carriage Return (like those created on a Macintosh), the lines appear merged together in a single line.

To add the proper character for the DOS Line Feed/ Carriage Return(LF/CR), Open the file in BBEdit, then click Save As and before saving, click Options and choose DOS line breaks.

Here are step-by-step instructions:

1. Save file from SAS window.

2. Open BBEdit (it's in Productivity & Other Tools>Viewers and Utilities).

3. Click File>Open and choose the file you want to convert.

4. Click File>Save As and choose a new file name (or you can click File>Save and save to the same name, if you wish).

5. Before saving, click Options, and then in the 'Line Breaks' field, choose DOS from the pull-down menu.

6. Click OK, and then save, to finish the conversion.

Question 86: Using e-macs instead of the SAS Program Editor in Interactive SAS

I would like to use e-macs when I'm in interactive SAS under UNIX, instead of the Program Editor.

How can I do this?

A: There are several ways to do this; all documented in the SAS Companion for the UNIX Environment, User Interfaces; The most straightforward way is to invoke SAS with the -editcmd switch, as follows:

```
sas -editcmd emacs
```

If you're using the X-Windows version of SAS, you need to specify the whole path to emacs, which is usually /usr/usc/bin/emacs, as in this example:

```
sas -editcmd /usr/usc/bin/emacs
```

Then, when you get into SAS, to start up an e-macs session, go to the command line of the Program Editor and type either:

```
Command==>  HOSTEDIT
```

Or

```
Command==>  HED
```

This opens a separate e-macs window where you edit the program you want, then when you close emacs, whatever you edited gets pasted into the Program Editor ready to submit or file (save) or edit further.

Question 87: Using Compressed Data Stored on UNIX Disk or UniTree

I am running out of space and want to compress my raw data files.

Can I access the data without uncompressing it? If yes, how is it done?

The compressed data are stored on:

1. UniTree
2. UNIX disk

A: SAS can access compressed raw data files using the PIPE feature of the FILENAME statement. Basically you will issue the UNIX uncompress command and have the uncompressed data feed into the SAS program.

Here are some examples:

1. Accessing compressed files on UniTree.

    Compressed raw data files do not have to be moved to UNIX disk to be used by SAS. The following code obtains raw data directly from a compressed file called 'full.housing.Z' stored on UniTree.

    ```
    filename raw pipe 'unitree get full.housing.Z - |
    uncompress ';

    data one;

    infile raw;

    input
    ```

    NOTE: The dash (-) in the FILENAME statement is not an error; it must appear, with a space before and after it, just as shown above.

The file 'full.housing.Z' never ends up on disk, so it will save a lot of time and space.

2. Accessing compressed local files.

    Local files can be accessed in the same manner as UniTree files with a slightly different filename statement. In this example we are trying to read the data in a file called 'crush.house1.Z' that is located in my directory called 'housing'.

    ```
    filename here pipe 'uncompress -c
    ~/housing/crush.house1.Z';
    data two;

    infile here;

    input
    ```

    The file 'crush.house1.Z' remains in compressed form in the 'housing' directory, saving time and space.

Question 88: Using Data Files Larger than 2 GB

UNIX systems using NFS protocols apparently have a 2 GB limit on the files they can handle.

How can I process data in any form that is in a file larger than 2 GB?

A: SAS allows creating and using files larger than 2 GB through a technique called partitioning. SAS breaks up the file for all UNIX operations, but considers it 'complete' for all SAS operations.

SAS advises that when using partition data sets, the following option should be included in config.sas:

```
-largefile sasvlfs
```

and that the file system being used for the partitions should be an xFS type file system. To check this, login to the machine and type 'mount';

To ask SAS to create partition data sets, define the partition size in a LIBNAME statement:

```
libname  abc  '/tmp/sasdata'  type=partition
partsize=1.6G;
```

The SAS data set (for example, xyz) will then be partitioned as follows:

```
xyz.ssd01.1, xyz.ssd01.2, etc.
```

But the SAS data set is referenced as any other SAS data set:

```
set abc.xyz
```

Note that whenever such a partitioned data set is used, you must use a LIBNAME statement with the TYPE= option specified, as in:

```
libname crsp '/wrdsx/crsp/sasdata' type=partition;
```

Here is an 'official' SAS Institute document on this topic.

SAS Solution for Large File Support on 32 bit UNIX Operating Systems.

Purpose:

This document will describe the usage of the WC appendage which will enable the SAS (c) system to access large files on 32-bit UNIX systems.

This will be accomplished via the partitioning of large datasets. These file partitions will be logically related and managed as one single file.

This capability will be available as an experimental option with SAS 6.11 TS040 on the Mips-ABI and Intel-ABI platforms. It will also be ported as an experimental option with SAS 6.12 for the SUN, IBM and HP UNIX workstations.

Use of Partitioned Libnames

The syntax for the partitioned libname is:

```
libname lname ('path1' [, 'path2' ...])
type=partition [partsize=#] ;
```

The paths may be either the names of existing directories or previously declared libnames, including other partitioned libnames.

For example:

```
libname p1 '/tmp/....';

libname p2 '/tmp/....';

libname p3 '/tmp/....';

libname part ('p1','p2','p3') type=partition;
```

and even:

```
libname part2 ('part','/tmp/....') type=partition
partsize=1.8g;
```

The libname 'part' consists of the three paths defined by the libnames 'p1', 'p2', and 'p3'. The libname part2 consists of the three paths defined for the libname 'part' and '/tmp/....' and specifies a partition size of 1.8Gig.

The partsize parameter specifies the size at which to split files. If part size is omitted, the default of 500Mb will be used. If partsize is specified, then the type parameter is optional as it will be assumed. The partsize can be specified in units of kilobytes (K), megabytes (M), or gigabytes (G). The default partition size can be changed using the new "-partsize" configuration option.

FUTURE ENHANCEMENT:

There is an incompatibility in the handling of the -partsize configuration option and the partsize libname option. The configuration option cannot handle decimal specifications such as 1.8G, and is currently producing inadequate error messages when such things are entered.

In the future, the code needs to handle such specifications, and produce better messages when garbage is entered.

On operating systems which allow file systems greater than 2Gb yet have single file limits of 2G it is allowable to specify the same path for all partitions.

Here's an example:

1) This example shows the use of partitioned libname on a system with two 2Gb drives mounted on the directories /disk1 and /disk2.
The SAS system can treat them as a single library with 3.6Gb of disk space using the following syntax:

```
libname example1 ('/disk1','/disk2') type=partition
partsize=1.8G
```

or

```
libname example1 ('/disk1','/disk2') partsize=1.8G
```

2) This example shows the use of partitioned libname on a system with one 5Gb drive mounted on the directory /diska. The SAS system can treat it as a single library with 4Gb of disk space portioned into 2Gb chunks using the following syntax:

```
libname example2 '/diska' type=partition partsize=2G
```

or

```
libname example2 '/diska' partsize=2G
```

Note that a single directory is given, and therefore the parenthesis syntax is not necessary. All partitions of a file will be placed in this single directory.

3) This example shows the use of partitioned libname on a system with one 640M drive mounted on the directory /diska and a previously declared libname with 500M. The SAS system can treat it as a single library with 1Gb of disk space partitioned into 500Mb chunks using the following syntax:

```
libname example3 ('/diska','otherlib') type=partition
```

or

```
libname example3 ('/diska','otherlib') partsize=500M
```

Note that the first libname uses the default partition size of 500M.

Naming of Partitions:

The SAS system will create one partition for each path specified. The first partition will reside in the first 'path' specified and has a normal SAS data set name (such as x.ssd01). Subsequent partitions reside in subsequent paths and have names in the form x.ssd01.1 where the trailing number increases with each partition. If an SAS file in a partitioned library is split into more partitions than directories supplied, an error message is written to the log, and processing of the step stops.
If a single path is supplied for a partitioned libname, all partitions are placed in this single directory.

This is useful on systems with Logical Volume Managers (LVMs) or extremely large disk drives to avoid the system management burden of keeping up with a file split into many partitions in many directories.

Partitioning the WORK Library:

Since the WORK library is heavily used by procs and the data step, it is sometimes necessary to partition it to support work files larger than 2Gb. Given two disk drives, /disk1 and /disk2 that a user wishes to use for WORK library processing, one would use the following syntax:

```
-work (/disk1,/disk2)
```

This line can be added to the config file or the command line of the SAS invocation (with appropriate shell escapes).

Note that the only way to adjust the partition size of the work library is to use the part size option.
The parentheses are the significant syntactic indicator to the parsing code that the work library is to be partitioned.

To obtain partitioning in a single directory (for LVM systems or large disk drives), you still have to use the parenthesis syntax:

```
-work (/diskbig)
```

Notes:

Some things to consider when using partitioned libnames include:

1) Consider the impact to backup and restore.

2) In environments where mixed size drives are used, the maximum partition size must fit on all drives. For example, if there is one 2G drive and one 640M drive, the maximum partition must fit within constraints of the 640M drive.

3) Previously existing work libraries cannot be attached to partitioned work libraries using the -noworkinit option.

Question 89: Floating Point Overflow Errors in PROC LOGISTIC

PROC LOGISTIC (aka PROC LOGIST) terminates with an error message as follows:

ERROR: Floating Point Overflow.

The SAS System stopped processing this step because of errors.

A: In most cases, the floating point overflow message in PROC LOGISTIC is a result of the maximum likelihood solution not existing. This will cause some of the parameters to become infinite and the procedure fails to converge. It is common for the maximum likelihood solution to not exist when there are few or no repeated observations at each observed setting of the covariates.

The solution to this problem is to either simplify the model or make the data denser by categorizing covariates.

Question 90: SAS Add-ons needs other SAS Modules to run Windows and Macintosh

Are there any other add-ons for the SAS System that I will use if I order any other add-ons for the SAS for Windows or SAS Macintosh such as SAS/EIS, SAS/QC, etc.?

ISSUE: Some SAS Add-ons require that other Add-ons (not just the BASE alone) be present in the system. All Add-ons must have SAS/BASE installed first. But, for example, SAS/EIS must also have the following modules installed: SAS/AF, SAS/FSP, and SAS/GRAPH.

A: If you are wondering what Add-ons are necessary for the functioning of certain parts of SAS, go into SAS for Windows or SAS for the Macintosh (you can do this in the User Rooms if you have not yet installed SAS on your system) and follow this clicking path:

Help (from the pull-down menu at the top of the screen)
Tech Support
Tech Support Main Page
Find your answer here
Technical Documents
SAS Technical Notes contained in this help application
Tech Talk
Product Dependencies

Question 91: Software that works with SAS

Is there any software that interfaces with SAS in various creative and useful ways?

A: This list, with descriptions, is not complete of course, and no endorsement is implied by virtue of something being included here.

Example: DBMS/Engines for Windows;

Functionality: Allows SAS programs to read and write data in a number of other proprietary formats, including Microsoft Access, Oracle, Sybase, Paradox, and others. Also reads and writes data used in other UNIX-based stat packages, including S-Plus, SPSS, Gauss, BMDP and Minitab, among others.

Platforms: MS Windows, Sun Solaris, and others.

Question 92: Selecting Observations in a Merge

Is it possible for SAS to include only the observations that came from one of the data sets or perhaps only observations that are present in both of the data sets or other combination when merging two or more data sets?

A: When merging SAS data sets, there is a data set option to create a temporary variable that 'flags' the observations that come from one or more of the data sets being merged.

The option (put in parentheses after the name of the data set being merged) is IN=X, where 'X' is the name of the temporary variable.

Observations that come from the data set so flagged will have a value of 1, and all others will have a zero. It looks like this:

```
data merged; merge ds1(in=a) ds2; by id;
```

 If you'd like to keep only observations that came from DS1, you can use the statement IF A; in the DATA step, as in this example:

```
data merged; merge ds1(in=a) ds2; by id; if a;
```

What the IF statement is really saying is: IF A EQ 1; Note that the above example keeps DS1 observations even if they are not present in DS2.

If you want to tell SAS to keep only observations that are present in both DS1 and DS2, you can use an IN= data set option on each of the data sets, then use a slightly more involved IF statement, as in this example:

```
data merged; merge ds1(in=a) ds2(in=b); by id; if a
and b;
```

What this IF statement is really saying is: IF A EQ 1 AND B EQ 1; You can even tell SAS to keep observations that are in one data set and not in the other (or any combination), as shown here:

```
data merged; merge ds1(in=a) ds2(in=b); by id; if not
a and b;
```

What this IF statement is really saying is: IF A NE 1 AND B EQ 1;

Here is a program you can run to try this out:

```
data ds1; input id height;

cards;

1 54

2 76

3 64

4 77
;

data ds2; input id weight;
cards;
1 154
2 177

3 103
4 203

5 156

6 227

7 113

;

data merged; merge ds1(in=a) ds2;

by id; if a;

proc print;

run;

OUTPUT:

The SAS System
```

```
OBS     ID      HEIGHT      WEIGHT
 1       1        54         154
 2       2        76         177
 3       3        64         103
 4       4        77         203
```

Question 93: Reading in to SAS data files with special delimiters

I have a TAB-delimited raw data file which is created using a spreadsheet program. TAB-delimited files are those in which the raw data values are separated by tabs instead of spaces.

SAS will not read the first column properly.

How do I get SAS to read the data properly?

A: Use of TAB-Delimited Data:

SAS can read tab-delimited files, although by default SAS assumes that blanks have been used to separate data values. You can get SAS to recognize different delimiters using the DELIMITER (or DLM) option in the INFILE statement.

The trick is to determine the correct value to use for TAB. TAB is represented in hexadecimal by '09'x in virtually all ASCII-based systems.

The following code will read the first four columns of a TAB delimited file:

```
DATA test;

Z='09'x;

INFILE 'tab.delimited.raw.file' DLM=Z;

INPUT one two three four;

<--more SAS code-->
```

NOTE: While the examples here use UNIX-type file references, the same examples can be used in other platforms by changing the file references to conform to the operating system conventions.

Although the above program appears to create the variable Z, because it is used as a delimiter it does not get saved in the SAS data set.

Sometimes, delimited data will have blank missing values which results in two delimiters side-by-side in the data file. If this is the case, the DSD option of the INFILE statement should be used so that SAS will avoid treating the two side-by-side delimiters as one.

Since the tab character cannot be shown in a text document like this, we'll use a "T" to represent the Tab in this example.

Note that in a real Tab-delimited file, you see empty space, not the letter "T".

54 T 75 T 253 T 44
87 T 3 T 55 T 465
905 TT 66 T 354

The DSD option has been added to recent Releases of SAS to deal with data coded like this. The following sample shows how use the dsd option to read tab-delimited data with blank missing values.

```
data temp; z='09'x; infile cards dsd dlm=z; input a b
c; cards; 54 T 75 T 253 T 44 87 T 3 T 55 T 465 905 TT
66 T 354 ; proc print data=temp; run;
```

Comma- and Quote-Delimited Data:

Other characters can be used as delimiters. For example, it is common to find data values separated by commas. SAS can read comma-delimited files, although by default SAS assumes that blanks have been used to separate data values. As explained above, you can get SAS to recognize different delimiters using the DELIMITER (or DLM) option in the INFILE statement.

Comma-delimited data may look something like this:

54,75,253,44
87,3,55,465
905,.,66,354

The following sample shows how to read comma-delimited data with the DLM= option.

```
data temp; infile cards dlm=',';
input a b c;
cards;

54,75,253,44
87,3,55,465
905,.,66,354

;

proc print data=temp;

run;
```

Again, note that sometimes delimited data may have blank missing values (which results in two delimiters side-by-side in the data file). If this is the case, the DSD option of the INFILE statement should be used so that SAS will avoid treating the two side-by-side delimiters as one. Comma-delimited data with quotes might look like this:

```
"54","75","253","44"
"87","3","55","465"
"905",".","66","354"
```

The following sample shows how use the dsd option to read comma-delimited data that also has quotes around each value.

```
data temp; infile cards dsd;

input a b c;

cards;

"54","75","253","44"
"87","3","55","465"
"905",".","66","354"

;
proc print data=temp;

run;
```

Quote-Delimited Data with Blank Missing Values

Sometimes, quote-delimited data (with other delimiters such as tabs or commas) has no character embedded to stand for a missing value. Instead of

"905",".","66","354"

you may have

"905","","66","354"

If you declare the comma and the quote as a missing value (you can specify more than one character when you use the DLM= option), SAS will strip off the quotes, and will have nothing left to indicate the missing value. To read this correctly, use a combination of the DLM= and DSD options, as in the following example:

```
data temp; infile cards dsd dlm=',';

input a b c;

cards;

"54","75","253","44"

"87","3","55","465"

"905","","66","354"
;

proc print data=temp;

run;
```

Question 94: Writing out from SAS data files with special delimiters

I have an SAS data set and I want to write out a TAB-delimited raw data file (such as those used in a spreadsheet program).

How do I get SAS to output the data with TAB separations?

A: Here's the solution:

Outputting TAB-Delimited raw Data:

SAS can write tab-delimited files, though the process is somewhat awkward. (SAS is promising that it will be much more elegant in Version 7, due out sometime in the future.)

The technique is to create a special variable that contains the character you want to use as a delimiter, and then specify this variable in the PUT statement between each of the actual variables you want to output.

Let's say you have an SAS data set with the following variables:

NAME AGE SEX SALARY

And you want SAS to output a TAB-delimited raw data file for use in some other software package.

Create a new variable using any name you haven't already used. Let's call it TABVAR.

The actual value for the TAB character is hex '09', so the assignment statement to create the new variable would be:

```
TABVAR = '09'x;
```

The standard method in SAS to output raw data is a DATA step with a FILE and a PUT statement.
This is documented in several of the locations noted at the end of this page.

Here is an example that assumes you have some data values in the SAS data set NONTAB and you want to output them to the file.

tabby.raw. The DATA _NULL_ statement is used because you don't need to make even a temporary SAS data set in the step that writes out the data, yet it is necessary to do this in a DATA step.

```
data _null_; set nontab;

tabvar='09'x;
file 'tabby.raw';
```

Put name tabvar age tabvar sex tabvar salary

The variable name TABVAR is arbitrary, and can be something as simple as TAB, or even T.

Outputting Comma-Delimited Data:

Other characters can be used as delimiters. For example, it is common to see data values separated by commas, and this kind of data is sometimes preferable in some other software packages.

Comma-delimited data may look something like this:

54,75,253,44
7,3,55,465
905,.,66,354

The statements needed to ask SAS to write out comma-delimited data are the same as those used for tab-delimited data, except that the tab variable (called TABVAR in the example above) is replaced with either a variable containing a comma or simply a comma, enclosed in quotes.

To use a variable that contains a comma, the assignment statement is used as follows:

```
COMMAVAR=',';
```

In the DATA step, then, the variable would be used like this:

```
data  _null_; set noncom;

commavar-',';

file 'commadel.raw';

put name commavar age commavar sex commavar salary;
```

The variable name COMMAVAR is arbitrary, and can be something as simple as COM, or even C.

When using a standard ASCII character such as a comma as your delimiter (unlike the TAB, which requires a HEX value as shown above), you also have the option of simply typing the delimiter in single quotes in the actual PUT statement, as shown in this:

Example:

```
data _null_; set noncom;
file 'commadel.raw';

put name ',' age ',' sex ',' salary;
```

Documentation:

Documentation and examples of the techniques outlined here are found in the SAS manuals, of course, and in the UCS documents 'SAS for Microcomputers' and 'SAS Under UNIX'.

Question 95: SAS across Different Systems

Do you have any overview document on SAS Transport Files?

A: SAS Transport Files:

People who have used SAS on other systems may well want to continue using the same SAS Data Sets on new platforms to which they will be moving. This document outlines and gives examples of the process of creating SAS Transport Files out of SAS Data Sets, moving these Transport Files to a new system, then reconverting the Transport Files into true SAS Data Sets on the new system.

NOTE: When moving to UNIX, it is possible to store SAS Transport Files as such in UniTree, and then access them directly from there. This is especially convenient for large data sets that would be impossible to store on disk and/or cumbersome to move back and forth from UniTree to UNIX disk for analysis.

SAS Transport Files -- Moving Between Systems

When moving between systems (not using SAS/CONNECT), it is necessary to prepare SAS Data Sets for the move, as simple transfer of true SAS Data Sets between operating systems will corrupt them.

Most types of SAS files, in fact, can be transferred from system to system, including Catalogs (such as Format Catalogs) as well as SAS Data Sets. Catalogs, however, cannot be transferred from one Release to a lower- numbered release (such as from 6.12 on UNIX to 6.08 on a mainframe).

Catalogs going to lower-numbered releases must be re-created on the target system using SAS code.

This document outlines the procedures for transferring SAS Data Sets, but the procedures for transfer of Catalogs, for example, are similar. Consult the appropriate SAS Manuals for details.

To accomplish the transfer of SAS Data Sets from one operating system to another it is necessary to

1. Convert the data set into "transport" format.

2. Move, send or carry the data in "binary" (i.e., non-translated) format to the operating system running the other Version.

3. Convert the transport data set back into an SAS Data Set.

"Transport format" here means that SAS writes out a standard ASCII data set that can be read by SAS running on other operating systems.

Some data transfer operations will require the use of documents that go beyond the one you are now reading. For one thing, it is important to note that the examples in this section assume moderate-sized data sets. Larger data sets may require increased space allocations or other manipulations when sending and/or receiving. Such manipulations are specific to the method of transfer or operating system(s) involved, and since the possibilities are quite numerous they cannot be documented here in detail. See related User's Manuals and documents for assistance.

Step One: Preparing the Data for the Move: Transport Format

Example 1: (Sending from UNIX)

```
libname olddata '/home/almaak/user12/sasdata'; **this
```
is the directory where the SAS Data Sets are;

```
filename guava '/home/almaak/user12/portfile.xpt';

proc cport data=olddata.mydata1 file=guava;
```

NOTE: as usual, if the file portfile.xpt is in the same directory where you invoked SAS, you don't need the path shown in the example. Also, you can substitute ~/ for your home directory in any path expression.

Example 2: (Sending from SAS for Windows)

```
libname olddata 'c:\sasdata';
```
**this is the directory where the SAS Data Sets are;

```
filename guava 'a:portfile.xpt';
```

```
proc cport data=olddata.mydata1 file=guava;
```

In these examples the location of the SAS Data Sets to be transferred is designated as old data and the file to which the transport version of the data is to be written is designated as guava, which is just a nickname (or FILEREF) for the actual file to be created on the A: drive, called portfile.xpt.

Step Two: Moving a Transport File to the Target System

Once the data are in transport format, the file may be moved by most methods appropriate for sending, copying or otherwise transferring ASCII data, provided that the sending method allows binary transfer (i.e., no translation takes place).

The file may be uploaded or downloaded between the PC and any system with pc-to-host communication packages, sent via eMail or bitnet, copied over PC-NFS, ftp'd, and so forth.

Step Three: Reconverting the Data to SAS Data Sets

Example 1: (Receiving at Windows)

If the receiving system is Windows, the transport file is identified by a FILENAME statement, and the permanent library is identified by a LIBNAME statement:

```
libname olddata 'c:\my\sasdata';
```
**SAS Data Sets will be written here;

```
filename cumquat 'a:portfile.xpt';
```

```
proc cimport library=olddata infile=cumquat;
```

The file from which the transport version of the data is to be read is designated as cumquat, which is just a nickname (or FILEREF) for the actual file portfile.xpt which for this example is shown on the diskette in

A:\. The location in which the SAS Data Set(s) will be written is designated as olddata.

PROC CIMPORT allows specifications other than LIBRARY to designate the output SAS Data Set location and name.

See the SAS documentation on PROC CIMPORT for details.

NOTE: Moving SAS data sets or catalogs from one Windows machine to another Windows machine requires no transport files. Files may simply be placed on a diskette or ZIP disk and carried or sent to the target machine. If you will be moving the files from one Windows machine to another Windows machine using eMail or ftp, however, transport files should be used anyway to avoid possible corruption.

Example 2: (Receiving at UNIX)

If the receiving system is UNIX, the transport file is identified by a FILENAME statement and the permanent library is identified by a LIBNAME statement:

```
libname olddata '/home/almaak/username';
```
**SAS Data Sets will be written here;

```
filename cumquat
'/home/almaak/username/portfile.xpt';
```

```
proc cimport library=olddata infile=cumquat;
```

This example shows file specifications in which the files and SAS data sets will reside in the "home" directory. (The "home" directory also may be represented with ~/.) The file from which the transport version of the data is to be read is designated as cumquat, which is just a nickname (or FILEREF) for the actual file previously placed in the "home" directory, and called portfile.xpt.

The location in which the SAS Data Set(s) will be written is designated as olddata. PROC CIMPORT allows specifications other than LIBRARY to designate the output SAS Data Set location and name.

See the SAS documentation on PROC CIMPORT for details.

Transport files created with PROC COPY:

Transport files in previous versions of SAS often were created using PROC COPY or a DATA step with an XPORT (or SASV5XPT) engine on a LIBNAME statement.
Files created in this way must be reconstructed using the same method.

Example 1: (Receiving at Windows, using PROC COPY):

libname   olddata   'c:\sasdata'; **SAS Data Sets are written here;

libname   pear   xport   'a:portfile.xpt';

proc copy in=pear out=olddata; select peach guava;

Example 2: (Receiving at UNIX, using PROC COPY):

libname olddata '/home/almaak/username'; **SAS Data Sets are written here;

libname   pear   xport
'/home/almaak/username/portfile.xpt';

proc copy in=pear out=olddata; select peach guava;

In Examples 1 and 2, "peach" and "guava" are SAS Data Sets "peach.sd2" and "guava.sd2" that will be written to the PC subdirectory "c:\sasdata" or "peach.ssd01" and "guava.ssd01" that will be written to the UNIX root directory.

The transported file is the Windows file "portfile.xpt" or the UNIX file "portfile.xpt", which is regarded as an SAS library with one or more (in this case two) members.

Example 3: (Receiving at Windows, using DATA step):

libname olddata 'c:\sasdata'; **SAS Data Sets are written here;

libname pear xport 'a:portfile.xpt';

data olddata.apple; set pear.peach;

Example 4: (Receiving at UNIX, using DATA step):

```
libname olddata '/home/almaak/username'; **SAS Data
```
Sets are written here;

```
libname pear xport
'/home/almaak/username/portfile.xpt';

data olddata.apple; set pear.peach;
```

The use of a DATA step, as shown in examples 3 and 4, allows the copying of only one SAS Data Set to the library specified (in this case OLDDATA), unlike the PROC COPY method (Examples 1/2) which allows the simultaneous importation of multiple SAS Data Sets.

Question 96: Recoding Variables with a Data Array

I have a number of similarly-coded variables, and I want to recode each of these variables using the same recoding scheme (e.g. 1=5 2=4 3=3 4=2 5=1). Can I recode the whole group of variables ISB1--ISB45 without having to refer to each variable separately?

Let's say you have three variables, A1, A2 and A3, and they all have values ranging from 1-20. You want to recode all three of these variables in exactly the same way:

```
old value   new variable's value
--------------------------------
1-5 = 1
6-15 = 2
16-20 = 3
```

A: SPSS SOLUTION:

This problem can be solved in SPSS with a VECTOR command.

Since my bias is to recode variables *into* new variables (rather than overwrite the existing information in the original variables), my example will allow for this by creating the new variables B1, B2 and B3 to contain the recoded (new) information.

Assume the original variables and information is in the SPSS active file. The following commands will modify the active file to contain the new (recoded) variables, as well as the original variables.

```
numeric b1 b2 b3 (F4.0).

vector multin = a1 to a3.

vector multout = b1 to b3.

loop #i=1 to 3.

do if multin(#i) ge 1 and multin(#i) le 5.
```

```
compute multout(#i)=1.
else if multin(#i) ge 6 and multin(#i) le 15.

compute multout(#i)=2.

else if multin(#i) ge 16 and multin(#i) le 20.

compute multout(#i)=3.

end if.

end loop.
```

* the following command is used to check the results.

```
list variables= a1 a2 a3 b1 b2 b3.

execute.
```

SAS SOLUTION:

This problem can be solved in SAS with the ARRAY statement, which is part of the DATA step.

Since my bias is to recode variables *into* new variables (rather than overwrite the existing information in the original variables), my example will allow for this by creating the new variables B1, B2 and B3 to contain the recoded (new) information.

Assume the original variables and information is in the SAS data set "original".

The following data step will create a new SAS data set called "nextstep" which will contain the recoded (as well as the original) variables.

```
data nextstep;  set original;

array prev{3} a1 a2 a3; * <--can also be written a1-
a3;

array new{3} b1 b2 b3;  * <--can also be written b1-
b3;

do i=1 to 3;
```

```
if prev{i} ge 1 and prev{i} le 5 then new{i} = 1;
if prev{i} ge 6 and prev{i} le 15 then new{i} = 2;

if prev{i} ge 16 and prev{i} le 20 then new{i} = 3;

end;

proc print data=nextstep;   * <--this is just to
check;

run;
```

Your "recoded" B1-B3 variables will then be available to use with
the new values.

Note that this procedure creates a new variable called "i" which
can be dropped if you wish.

Question 97: Changing the Internal Order of Variables in an SAS Data Set

How can I make SAS data set in order when I use PROC PRINT without a VAR statement?

A: In a new DATA step, use one of the following BEFORE a SET statement: ATTRIB, ARRAY, FORMAT, INFORMAT, and LENGTH, RETAIN.

Each of these statements sets up the variable order in the input data vector for the new SAS data set, and the set statement then copies the variables into the new order.

For example:

```
data temp;
input c a b;
cards;
8
4
6
9
3
6
8
6
2
;
data temp2;

length a b c 4;

set temp;

proc print;
run;
```

Question 98: Selecting a given word from a Variable Value

How do I select a given word from a variable value?

A: To select a word from a variable value, use the SCAN function to specify which part of the value you want and the delimiter that separates the parts.

Here is an example:

```
data a;

x='this is the example';

y=scan(x,2,' ');

run;
```

In this example, Y has a value of "is".

Question 99: Converting SAS Files for use in Version 9.1 -- PROC MIGRATE

How can I convert SAS File for Version 9.1?

A: Some SAS Data Sets and other SAS Files must be converted for use in Version 9.1 if they were created in earlier versions. The Procedure provided by SAS for this purpose is PROC MIGRATE.

Note that PROC MIGRATE does not work on all Version 8 files. Attempted conversion of some files will result in the message:

ERROR: <catalog or data set name> was created under a different operating system

In most cases, this probably refers to the difference between the 32-bit operating system under which Version 8.x was running and the 64-bit operating system under which Version 9.x runs. Regardless of the specific reason, the solution virtually always is to use PROC CPORT/PROC CIMPORT to do the conversion.

SAS Institute has explained the situation to us as follows:

SAS 9 users can safely interchange data files with SAS 8 users under certain circumstances. The most straight forward example of interchanging data files with an SAS 8 user is one where the SAS 9 data file is created and used in an SAS 8 session within the same operating system family. It is therefore, considered native to the operating system.

As long as features have not been used which were not available in the prior version, such as long format names, this file can be used "as is".

SAS 9 was released under certain UNIX platforms as a 64 bit application. If you run SAS in a 64 bit environment, then create an SAS 9 data set and try to read it in an SAS 8 session running in a 32 bit environment on the same machine, Cross Environment Data Access (CEDA) will enable you to use the data set with certain restrictions.

Catalogs cannot be accessed at all without cporting them to transport format and cimporting them into the SAS 8 session. Bear in mind, cport will only work for catalogs, in this instance.

As a general rule, cport is used to move data sets and catalogs from one release to the same release or higher.

If CEDA is used to translate the file, you cannot update it. When you process the file, you may notice a slight reduction in performance. Also, CEDA does not support indexing and will not use any index associated with the file. You can confirm whether CEDA is being used to read the file, by first setting the system option MSGLEVEL=I, then, running a procedure on all or some of the observations in the data set. You can also run PROC CONTENTS in an SAS 9 session.

Under the field DATA REPRESENTATION, you will see 'foreign' if it is anything other than the operating system you are using.

The message in the log using MSGLEVEL=i, follows if CEDA is being used.

INFO: Data set is in a foreign host format. Cross Environment Data Access will be used, which may require additional CPU resources and reduce performance.

If you've confirmed that CEDA is being used to process the data file, you can use PROC COPY with the NOCLONE option to copy it and remove the processing restrictions.

Here is an example.

```
libname noCEDA 'path-to-folder-containing-foreign-file';

PROC COPY IN=noCEDA OUT=temp NOCLONE;

/*Make sure to use the SELECT statement */

/*otherwise, the whole library will be copied */

SELECT dsname;

UN;
```

You can also use the DATA STEP. When you create a new data set, it will be created in the native data representation of the operating system under which you are currently running and remove the CEDA restrictions.

Here is an example.

```
DATA new;

SET dsname;

RUN;
```

Question 100: Setting FTP download mode in SAS

How do I set FTP download mode in SAS?

A: You can programmatically set the FTP download mode in SAS.

Specifying multiple RCMD options on FILENAME statement not supported with FTP filename engine

When using the FTP access method and specify multiple RCMD options on the FILENAME statement, the assignment fails due to the multiple RCMD values being overlaid. Specifying multiple RCMD options on the FILENAME statement is not supported.

The only method available to send multiple commands is through the SITE FTP command.

The SITE command allows multiple arguments.

For instance, to set the RDW option and binary transfer mode, code the RCMD option in the following way:

```
rcmd='site rdw recfm=s'
```

Both RDW and RECFM are parameters to the FTP SITE command.

To see all available parameters, submit:

```
rcmd='help site'
```

Question 101: Reading SAS Data Sets in SAS Release 7

SAS Release 7 cannot read SAS Data Sets created in Version 6.04 (SAS-PC for DOS). SAS Release 6.04 Data Sets have the DOS file extension .ssd. This is one of the first times SAS has distributed a product that is not compatible with all previous formats of data storage.

A: If Version 6 (Release 6.08 or above) is available, convert the .ssd file to an .sd2 file using a variant of the following:

```
libname in v604 'c:\mysaspc';

libname out v612 'c:\mysaswin';

proc copy in=in out=out;
```

It is not necessary to use the v604 and v612 engines; they are placed in the example for purposes of explicitness.

Note that ONLY SAS 6.04 (.ssd) Data Sets should be in the first directory (c:\mysaspc in the example), and there should be no .ssd files in the second directory (c:\mysaspc in the example). In other words, keep the SAS data sets of the two types (.ssd and .sd2) separated in their respective places.

If Version 6 is not available, the process is a bit more involved. First, go to the SAS Web site and download the SAS System Viewer. This software is a free package that is included with the SAS System on the CD distributed by ITS, but the Web site will have the most recent version, and installation is probably easier this way.

1. Go to http://www.sas.com/

2. Click Demos/Downloads (left of page, under Software).

3. Find 'SAS System Viewer' in the 'Downloads Sorted Alphabetically' field (top of page).

4. Follow instructions to download and install the Viewer.

5. Launch the Viewer, and click Open to load the .ssd file.

6. Click 'Save as File' and choose your favorite format (comma-delimited .csv is recommended).

7. Open SAS Version 7 or higher and read in the newly saved file using the Import Wizard.

Question 102: Special considerations in Release 7 and higher

The newer versions of SAS (Version 7 and higher) are completely compatible with data and programs from the past.

Is there any detailed information and suggestions for moving to the higher versions?

A: SAS changed the structure of SAS data sets in Release 7, as compared with prior releases of the system. SAS data sets created in prior releases will be readable in Release 7 and higher, but those created in 7 and higher will not be usable in previous Releases. In other words, SAS data sets are upwardly, but not downwardly, compatible with respect to Release 7 and beyond.

If you have SAS data sets created prior to release 7, SAS can read most of them in later versions without special attention, but it may be to your advantage to convert your SAS data sets for use in Version 7 or later. It is possible in many cases to make conversions without using any SAS engines, since the default engine for new SAS data sets is the one appropriate for the most recent version, and SAS automatically uses the appropriate engine for any SAS data sets it needs to read.

In SAS documentation, however, the engines are specified, so these examples will follow that style.

Some of the following steps are recommended, some required, in converting SAS data sets, and each step is so labeled.

1. Make a new subdirectory (folder) to contain the SAS data sets being created under the new version of SAS. For example, you might have your 6.12 SAS data sets in a directory called sasdata, and you might create a new directory called v8data to store the new data sets.

2. (Required) Run some version of the following SAS program to create new SAS data sets from your old ones:

UNIX example:

```
libname old v612 '~/sasdata';

libname new v8 '~/v8data';

proc copy in=old out=new;

Windows example:

libname old v612 'c:\sasdata';

libname new v8 'c:\v8data';

proc copy in=old out=new;
```

In SAS for Macintosh, the DOS subdirectory/folder specification in the example above should be replaced by the usual Macintosh folder syntax.) The engines in these examples may be unnecessary as explained above, or may need to be changed to match the Versions that created the SAS data sets in your particular situation.

3. Once you are satisfied that the conversion was successful, you can delete the 6.12 versions of your SAS data sets from ~/sasdata (or c:\sasdata).

If your SAS data sets were created under Version 6.04 (SAS-PC, or SAS for DOS) or earlier, they cannot be converted directly to Version 7 or beyond. They must be converted first to Version 6.12, then from Version 6.12 to Version 7 or later.

Question 103: Database Permissions to run Scheduler

What database permissions are required for the id that is used to run the Scheduler?

A: The batch Scheduler userid must be granted the following permissions:

GRANT SELECT ON <schema owner>.ISMFLDCT TO <db logon>

GRANT SELECT ON <schema owner>.ISMDBSTR TO <db logon>

GRANT SELECT ON <schema owner>.ISMCONFIG TO <db logon>

GRANT SELECT ON <schema owner>.ISMVERSN TO <db logon>

GRANT SELECT ON <schema owner>.ISMDBINF TO <db logon>

GRANT SELECT, DELETE, UPDATE, INSERT ON <schema owner>.ISMTASKSCHED TO <db logon>

GRANT INSERT ON <schema owner>.ISMREMINDERS TO <db logon>

GRANT SELECT, DELETE, UPDATE, INSERT ON <schema owner>.ISMExportCtrl TO <db logon>

Question 104: Array Statements

ARRAY statements that used to work under Version 6 don't work now in Version 7, 8 or 9. The error message may be, 'Cannot Find a Library containing Subroutine XXX'.

A: The syntax for ARRAY statements in PROC PHREG has changed; although the syntax for ARRAY statements in DATA steps remains the same as before. SAS Note SN-000541 documents this change in syntax, and reads (in part) as follows:

The array syntax used in PROC PHREG has changed. You must use braces { } when you define an array:

array pp{*} P1-P15; You must use brackets [ ]when you refer to an array element: if ll[i] <= Time < ll[i]+1 then NPap= pp[i];

The "braces" mentioned in the note are the characters that are also called curly-brackets. They are not regular parentheses.

Question 105: Estimating the distribution of sample data

Can I estimate the distribution (mass or density function) of my observed sample data?

A: Yes, you can estimate the distribution of your observed sample data. Two methods are available:

*Parametric density estimation: You select a distribution (such as normal or exponential) and the parameters of the distribution are estimated.

*Kernel density estimation: This is a nonparametric method that uses a kernel function and a smoothing parameter.

From the Distribution(Y) results window, select either Curves: Parametric Density or Curves: Kernel Density.

This can also be done using the distribution options in the HISTOGRAM statement of Base SAS PROC UNIVARIATE or SAS/QC PROC CAPABILITY.

Question 106: Using Version 7

Version 7 and later SAS Data Sets and Catalogs are not compatible (cannot be used) with Version 6.12.
For most users who convert their work to Version 7 and beyond, this will not be a concern, but those who might need to return to Version 6, or share their data with colleagues who only have access to Version 6, this incompatibility will be problematic.

On the (somewhat) bright side, Versions 7 and 8, as well as 9 for Windows (but not UNIX) can read and write (create) Version 6 SAS Data Sets and Catalogs, so there are alternatives for most users;

SUMMARY:

Version 7, 8 and 9 Data Set file extension: .sas7bdat
Version 7, 8 and 9 Catalog file extension: .sas7bcat

Version 6 (UNIX) Data Set file extension: .ssd01
Version 6 (UNIX) Catalog file extension: .sct01

Version 6 (Windows/Mac) Data Set file extension: .sd2
Version 6 (Windows/Mac) Catalog file extension: .sc2

Version 6.04 (DOS) Data Set file extension: .ssd
Version 6.04 (DOS) Catalog file extension: .sct

Compatibility Table:

Version 7,8,9   Version 6.12

.sas7bdat
yes

no
.sas7bcat
yes

no
.ssd01 (UNIX)
yes

yes
.sct01 (UNIX)
yes

yes
.sd2 (Win/Mac)
yes

yes
.sc2 (Win/Mac)
yes

yes
.ssd (DOS)
no

yes
.sct (DOS)
no

yes

A: Users who might want to go back to Version 6, either for their own work or when sharing work with colleagues, should use Version 6 "engines" when creating permanent SAS Data Sets and Catalogs, even when using Version 7 or above. This is done by specifying the V612 engine in a LIBNAME statement, as in this example:

```
libname xyz v612 '~/sasfiles';
```

Where xyz is an arbitrary nickname of your choice, and ~/sasfiles is an example of whatever location you choose for your permanent SAS data sets.

NOTE: If you are using both Version 6 and Version 7 (or later) SAS Data Sets, they must be stored in different subdirectories (SAS calls these "Libraries").

In this situation, you would use two different LIBNAME statements with the V612 engine specified only on one of them.

Question 107: Determining the polygon selected point

Is there a way within SAS/GIS to determine which polygon a selected point lies within?

A: Yes, there is. You need to define a lattice for your map and use a feature within SAS/GIS called Set Area Attributes in order to determine which polygon a point that you have selected is located within.
The Set Area Attributes feature assigns an area value to points in your map.

Do the following:

Step 1: Open the SASUSER.MALL.AREA map in the GIS Map window.

Step 2: Make the TRACT layer selectable by clicking the right mouse button over the TRACT layer name in the layer bar and selecting "Make Layer Selectable".

Step 3: Make the SCHOOL layer selectable by clicking the right mouse button over the SCHOOL layer name in the layer bar and selecting "Make Layer Selectable".

Step 4: Select any tracts and schools. To select multiple items, use one of the select tools in the GIS Tool palette or hold down the SHIFT key and click on the items.

Step 5: Create a new spatial from the selected items. From the GIS Map window, select:

File ==> Save As ==> Spatial

In the GIS Spatial Save Options window, enter the following:

Output Spatial and Data Sets

Library: SASUSER Catalog: TRACTS Spatial: TRACTS

Chains: TRACTSC Nodes: TRACTSN Details: TRACTSD

Subset Data by:
X Selected Items

Project Coordinates Using:
X Lat/Lon

Select OK.

Step 6: In order to create a new SAS/GIS map consisting of the selected items that is independent of the original map, you will need to recreate the catalog entries and data sets that SAS/GIS uses to draw the map. Submit the following statements from the SAS Program Editor to accomplish this task:

```
PROC GIS CATALOG=SASUSER.TRACTS;

SPATIAL TRACTS;
```

Define the coverage entry for the new map.

```
COVERAGE REPLACE TRACTS / WHERE='1';
```

Define the composite for the variables that define the TRACT area layer.

```
COMPOSITE REPLACE TRACT / CLASS=AREA VAR=(TRACTL
TRACTR);
```

Define the polygonal index to identify the polygons for the TRACT area layer.

```
POLYGONAL INDEX REPLACE TRACT / OUT=SASUSER.TRACTPI

COMPOSITE=TRACT;
```

Define the TRACT area layer entry.

```
LAYER REPLACE TRACT / TYPE=AREA COMPOSITE=TRACT;
```

Define the SCHOOL point layer entry.

```
LAYER REPLACE SCHOOL / TYPE=POINT
WHERE='CLASS="scho"';

RUN;
```

Define the new map entry that contains the TRACT and
SCHOOL layers.

```
MAP REPLACE TRACT / LAYERS=(TRACT SCHOOL) LATLON
DETAILS

COVERAGE=TRACTS;

RUN;

QUIT;
```

Step 7: Open the SASUSER.TRACTS.TRACT map in the GIS
map window. The new map containing the selected tracts and
schools will be displayed.

Please note that you may have to turn the SCHOOL layer on by
selecting the check box to the left of the SCHOOL layer name in
the layer bar before the school points will be visible on the map.

Question 108: Making Windows stay in foreground

How can I make windows stay in the foreground that are displayed when an action is performed (such as an FSBROWSE, FSVIEW, or GRAPH window)?

A: On PC platforms, when you perform a GIS action that displays another window, such as a GRAPH or FSBROWSE window, that window is hidden behind the GIS Map window. To make the window stay on top of the GIS Map window after an action is performed, issue a DM statement to bring that window to the foreground.

For example, instead of using the BROWSE action, define a PROGRAM action to bring up the FSBROWSE window, and keep this window active by including the following DM command:

DM GIS 'FSBROWSE data-set-name <screen-name>' FSB;

You can also issue the DM statement to make sure that the GRAPH1 window remains on top of the GIS Map window after submitting a graphics procedure in a PROGRAM action. Add the following DM statement to the bottom of the code:

```
DM GIS 'GRAPH1' GRAPH1;
```

The window name at the end of the DM statement specifies the window that will be active after the command has executed.

Question 109: Adding label to the new point

I have a point layer on my SAS/GIS map that already contains labels. If I add a new point to the layer, its label is not automatically added to the map.

How can I add a label to the new point?

A: Labels in SAS/GIS are static in the sense that each label is an observation in a label data set.

Adding a new point does not automatically add a new observation to your label data set for that point. However, you do not have to delete all of your existing labels and re-create them in order to have a label added to your new point.

Follow these steps:

1. Invoke SAS/GIS, and open your map.

2. Select all of the new, unlabeled points on your map.

3. Select Edit==>Add Labels...from the GIS Map window.

4. In the GIS Add Labels window, under 'Apply label to:' choose 'Selected Items'. Continue to select the other label parameters, including Text Options and Font, and click OK. The new points should now be labeled. When you exit the map and save the label data set, observations for the new labels will be added.

Question 110: Scheduler Parameters

What are the scheduler parameters?

A: "[directory path]\SchedEngine.exe"
DSN=Sched;UID=sm;PWD=sm, <SchemaName>, <EngineID>,
<MaxTasks>

* The part in the double quotation marks is the OS path to the scheduling engine executable file and will be different on each customer site.

* The part after that and before the first comma is the ODBC database name and database login and password will be different on each Customer site.

* The information after the first comma is the database schema that you want to use. This is only necessary if after logging into Campaign Management you get the Choose Database Schema dialog box. This can be left blank.

* The information after the second comma is the scheduling engine ID used if you configure multiple schedulers on the same machine. It is important that this is different for each shortcut. It is best to use a character entry here rather than a number, as this information gets stored in the event log at each step and will therefore clearly identify which scheduler did what.

* The last one is the maximum number of tasks to pick-up at any one time and this too can be left blank.

Question 111: Formats that export files can use

What formats can export files use?

A: Export files can use fixed text format or delimited. They can be formats saved as a database table on the server (Export to database), saved as a text file on the client Machine (Export to local file), saved as a text file on the server box (Export to file on server), or appended to an existing file.

Question 112: Installing SAS for Windows

When I install SAS for Windows, it cannot get past the Setinit procedure, giving error related page faults, o'x' exceptions and the VWIN32 module.

A: Most likely, the cause of these errors is a slightly modified version of Windows 95 that newer computers have built in. The original Windows 95 version is 4.00.950A. The slightly modified Version appears as 4.00.950B

To see what version of Windows 95 you are running, click the right mouse button on 'My Computer', and go to 'Properties'.

SAS offers two solutions to this problem. You can either return to Windows 95 Version 4.00.950A, or you can download a Fiber Fix from SAS Institute that allows SAS to run with Windows 95 Version 4.00.950B.

To return to 4.00.950A, go to Start>Settings>Control Panel, and choose Add/Remove Programs, then highlight 'USB Supplement to OSR2' and select 'Remove'.

Question 113: Creating Version 6.12 SAS Data Set

Version 7, 8 and 9 SAS Data Sets cannot be used in SAS prior to Version 7, but there are reasons to use Version 7, 8 or 9 data in Version 6, especially during a time of transition to the higher versions.

For example, you may be using Version 8 in your work, but you want to share data with a colleague who is still using Version 6.12.

NOTE that as of Version 9, SAS is beginning to withdraw support of Version 6 data sets.

In SAS for Windows, a warning appears stating that future versions "may not" be able to create or update Version 6 SAS Data Sets. In UNIX, Version 9 already does not allow creation or updating of Version 6 SAS Data Sets.

A: To create a Version 6.12 SAS data set or Catalog from a Version 8 SAS data set or Catalog, create a new subdirectory (folder), then specify a separate LIBNAME statement for that new subdirectory (folder) -- which SAS calls a Library -- and add the v612 engine.

```
libname xyz v612 '~/sas6lib'; /*<--UNIX example **/

libname xyz v612 'c:\sas6lib'; /*<--Windows
example**/

libname xyz v612 'Hard_Disk:Sas6Lib'; /*<--Macintosh
example**/
```

Where xyz is an arbitrary nickname of your choice, and sas6lib is an example of the location you have set up for your Version 6 files.

NOTE that when you are using both Version 6 and Version 7 (or later) SAS Data Sets, they must be stored in different Libraries (subdirectories, folders). In this situation, you would use two different LIBNAME statements with the V612 engine specified only on one of them.

After your two LIBNAME statements have been submitted, you can then use PROC COPY or a DATA step to create the new (Version 6) data set or catalog. Here are two complete examples:

DATA STEP Example:

```
libname abc 'c:\v8files';

libname xyz v612 'c:\sas6lib';

data xyz.oranges; set abc.oranges;
```

PROC COPY Example:

```
libname abc 'c:\v8files';

libname xyz v612 'c:\sas6lib';

proc copy in=abc out=xyz;
```

If you are making a transport file to move your data or catalogs to another type of system (e.g., Windows to UNIX), you need to create a so-called "Version 5" transport file using PROC COPY and a LIBNAME statement with the XPORT engine.

Question 114: SAS under UNIX Release 7

SAS under UNIX Release 7 and beyond doesn't work in a telnet or xterm, or other character-based window like it did with Version 6.12 and earlier.

A: Unfortunately, the only solutions at the present time are:

1. Use X-Windowing software on any microcomputer that is connecting to your USC account to run SAS.

    * Mac X11 (Macintosh) and Micro-X (Windows) are available in Public User Rooms;

    * Micro-X is available for site-license purchase from ITS.

2. Run SAS from a Sun Workstation (e.g., in one of the Public User Rooms) that is running an X-Windowing system.

3. Use SAS Under UNIX only in Batch Mode (see the section titled: "Batch Processing" in the ITS Help Document SAS Under UNIX for more information).

    SAS Institute is considering WWWeb-based solutions that might allow SAS Version 7 or higher to be accessed through a browser. If and when more information becomes available, it will be posted at this site.

Question 115: Changing name of a layer on SAS/GIS map

How can I change the name of a layer on my SAS/GIS map?

A: There are two methods for changing a layer name in SAS/GIS.

Method 1: To rename the layer interactively, follow these steps:

1. Invoke SAS/GIS and open your map.

2. Edit the layer definition for the layer that you want to rename by clicking with the right mouse button   over the layer name in the Layer Bar and selecting 'Edit Layer Definition'.

3. Select File => Rename. . .from the GIS Layer window.

4. Enter the new name of the layer, and click OK. The new layer name will appear in the Layer Bar.

Method 2: To rename the layer in batch, use the RENAMELAYER option in the MAP UPDATE statement in PROC GIS, as in the following example.

Note that parameters in the code below that are in uppercase are required syntax, and lowercase parameters need to be replaced with values specific to your spatial data base.

```
PROC GIS CATALOG=libref.catalog;

SPATIAL spatial-entry-name;

MAP UPDATE map-entry-name / RENAMELAYER old-layer-name = new-layer-name ;

RUN;
QUIT;
```

Please note that the RENAMELAYER option is not documented in SAS/GIS Software: Usage and Reference.

Question 116: Equation for a nonparametric regression model

How can I get the equation for a nonparametric regression model so that I can generate predicted values for a new data set?

A: Nonparametric models can be fit via the GAM, LOESS, and TPSPLINE procedures and in SAS/INSIGHT (use Analyze: Fit followed by selecting Spline, Kernel, or Loess from the Curves menu). Nonparametric models cannot be represented with a simple equation as can regression and linear models from such procedures as REG, GLM, GENMOD, and others.

As a result, there is no simple set of parameter estimates that can be saved in a data set and reused at a later time in a prediction equation to score new data.

Predictions for new data are done as the nonparametric model is fit via the SCORE statement in the GAM, LOESS, and TPSPLINE procedures. For example, these statements fit a spline model in PROC GAM, score the observations in the VALIDATE data set, and save them in the PREDS data set:

```
proc gam data=training;

model y = spline(x);

score data=validate out=preds;

run;
```

In SAS/INSIGHT, scoring can be done either interactively in the Fit window after the model is fit, or as a batch as the model is fit.

In either case, select Vars: Predicted Curves: type, where type is the same (Spline, Kernel, Loess, or Local Polynomial) as you previously selected from the Curves menu to fit the nonparametric model, and then complete the resulting dialog box identically to the corresponding Curves dialog box.

This adds a new column (such as PS_response for a spline fit) that contains predicted values from the nonparametric model to the data table.

Note that the P response column contains predicted values from the parametric model.

Next, enter a period (missing value) in a new row of the data table in the response variable's column and specify the desired values for each of the predictors that are used in the model. Press the TAB or ENTER key to compute the predicted values (parametric and nonparametric) for this new row.

To score a data set as a batch, concatenate the new data to the original data and set the response variable for the new observations to missing. Then fit the model in SAS/INSIGHT and create predicted values via the Vars: Predicted Curves menu as described above.

The added observations will not affect the model fit because observations with missing response values are ignored, but predicted values will be computed for all observations for which the predictors are not missing.

Question 117: Rearranging Data

I have some data arranged in multiple observations per person (not necessarily the same number of observations for each) and I want to move all data for one person into one observation.

This problem is different in that each person doesn't have a grade for each of the possible outcome columns, so some values in the resulting matrix will be missing.

Name the ID number and three variables (NAME, COURSE and GRADE). Each observation represents a different course attended by a person in the study. Each person has up to four grades, but there are six possible courses represented in the data.

How can I rearrange data so that each person's data are stored in a single observation instead of multiple observations per person?

A: Original data structure for the example is 8 observations representing 2 subjects, and four variables: ID, NAME, and COURSE GRADE. The goal is to have two observations (one for each person) and 8 variables: ID, NAME, G110 (grade for course called BISC110), G201, G330, G410, G215, G395.

EXAMPLES: Original data for Method 2 look like:

```
ID    NAME    COURSE    GRADE

004   Smith   BISC110   A-
004   Smith   BISC201   B+
004   Smith   BISC330   A
004   Smith   BISC410   A-
012   Jones   BISC110   B-
012   Jones   BISC215   C-
012   Jones   BISC330   A-
012   Jones   BISC395   A
```

SPSS Example (Method 2):

In this example, we want one column (variable) representing each different COURSE to contain the original GRADE values, and one row (observation) representing each ID (person). We read the data in and create the active file.

```
data list free / id * name (a10) course (A7) grade
(A2).
begin data.

004   Smith   BISC110   A-
004   Smith   BISC201   B+
004   Smith   BISC330   A
004   Smith   BISC410   A-
012   Jones   BISC110   B-
012   Jones   BISC215   C-
012   Jones   BISC330   A-
012   Jones   BISC395   A

end data.
```

We create one new variable for each COURSE.

```
string g110 g201 g330 g410 g215 g395 (a2).
```

We set the value of each course column to MISSING when it's the
first row (observation) in each ID group, This is necessary
because later we will be asking SPSS to keep each grade value
once it's placed in a column, until the last row (observation) for
each ID group, and then we'll select out only that last row
for our final data set.

If we don't set the new course columns to missing at the
beginning of each ID number group, SPSS will keep grades from
previous ID numbers (people), which we don't want.

```
do if id ne lag(id).
+ compute g110=" ".
+ compute g201=" ".
+ compute g330=" ".
+ compute g410=" ".
+ compute g215=" ".
+ compute g395=" ".
end if.
```

Here we tell SPSS to record the grade for each course in the
corresponding new column representing that original course.

```
if (course="BISC110") g110=grade.
if (course="BISC201") g201=grade.
if (course="BISC330") g330=grade.
```

```
if (course="BISC410") g410=grade.
if (course="BISC215") g215=grade.
if (course="BISC395") g395=grade.
```

Here is where we tell SPSS to keep (repeat) each grade in the column once it's read in, so that by the last row for each ID number, all grades for that ID number (person) will be present.

```
do if id eq lag(id).
+ if (g110=" ") g110=lag(g110).
+ if (g201=" ") g201=lag(g201).
+ if (g330=" ") g330=lag(g330).
+ if (g410=" ") g410=lag(g410).
+ if (g215=" ") g215=lag(g215).
+ if (g395=" ") g395=lag(g395).
end if.
```

Here, by a strange little trick, we use MATCH FILES (even though we're using only one file) to create a LAST variable, which enters a 1 as the value for the last ID number in each group. (If the data are unsorted, they must be sorted BY ID before this is done).

```
match files file=* / by=id / last=breaker.
```

The remaining statements select only the last observation for each ID number (person) and, via the SAVE command, DROPs variables that we don't need anymore.

```
select if breaker=1.
save outfile='final' / drop grade breaker.
execute.
```

The data then look like this:

ID	NAME	COURSE	G110	G201	G330	G410	G215	G395
4.00	Smith	BISC410	A-	B+	A	A-		
12.00	Jones	BISC395	B-		A-		C-	A

SAS Example (Method 2):

This example reads grades assigned in particular courses, and then reorganizes the data so that each course has its own column containing all the grades in that course, and each person has only one row (observation) showing all their grades.

```
data one;
input id name $ course $ grade $;
cards;
004 Smith BISC110 A-
004 Smith BISC201 B+
004 Smith BISC330 A
004 Smith BISC410 A-
012 Jones BISC110 B-
012 Jones BISC215 C-
012 Jones BISC330 A-
012 Jones BISC395 A
;

/*** sort BY ID to create FIRST.ID and LAST.ID
variables, used later ***/

proc sort data=one out=two; by id;
```

In this DATA step, the new variables (G110, G201, &c.) are set to missing at the beginning of each ID number group (i.e., on the first observation of each person), and by using the RETAIN keyword, once each grade is assigned to its new column, it remains in that column until the end of that ID number group (i.e., until the last observation of each person) ***/

```
data three; set two; by id; drop grade;
retain g110 g201 g330 g410 g215 g395;
 if first.id then do;
 g110=" "; g201=" "; g330=" "; g410=" "; g215=" ";
g395=" ";
 end;
 if course="BISC110" then g110=grade;
 else if course="BISC201" then g201=grade;
 else if course="BISC330" then g330=grade;
 else if course="BISC410" then g410=grade;
 else if course="BISC215" then g215=grade;
 else if course="BISC395" then g395=grade;
 if last.id;
run;
```

The data then are arranged as follows:

OBS	ID	NAME	COURSE	G110	G201	G330	G410	G215	G395
1	4	Smith	BISC410	A	B	A	A		
2	12	Jones	BISC395	B		A		C	A

**/

Question 118: Reading the rest of Variables

Some data files have information given in some of the early variables as to how the rest of the variables should be read in. This is not as simple as checking to see what a LINETYPE is and then using a different INPUT statement based on what you find (like the Census PUMS files, in which either a line is a Household record [LINETYPE='H'] or a Person record [LINETYPE='P']).

This is a situation in which values in a particular observation will be read into different variables depending on what values are found early in the INPUT line.

A: Here is an example: Let's say you have data for various months of the year but the months in which you have data are different for each employee. Mary has data for months 3 through 7, John for months 2 through 5, and Patt for months 4 through 9.

Use an ARRAY that specifies the lowest possible month (2) and the highest possible month (9), and then have the DO loop start with the BEGIN value and end with the END value that are read in at the beginning of the INPUT sequences for each employee (i.e., each observation).

```
/**************************************************/

data test(drop=I);

infile cards;

array v{2:9} v2-v9;

input emplname $4. begin 6 end 9 @;

do i = begin to end;

input v{i} @;

end;

cards;
```

```
Mary 3   7    5 2 3 5 3

John 2   5    7 5 6 4

Patt 4   9    2 7 6 8 3 4

;

proc print;

run;
```

```
/****************************************************
```
This program also works if the data following the employee name
line are on more than one record, but it is crucial that you have
exactly the right number of data values on the following lines as
are specified in the BEGIN -- END range.
```
****************************************************/
data test(drop=I);

infile cards;

array v{2:9} v2-v9;

input emplname $4. begin 6 end 9 @;

do i = begin to end;

input v{i} @;

end;

cards;

Mary 3   7
5 2
3 5 3
John 2   5

7 5 6 4
Patt 4   9

2 7
6 8
3 4
;

proc print;
```

```
run;
```

Question 119: Repetitive DATA steps

Repetitive DATA steps take a lot of time when dealing with large data matrices.

How can I resole this?

A: SAS can do DATA step operations in RAM memory if permanent SAS Data Sets are not being written. Increase the RAM on your computer and use temporary SAS Data Sets whenever possible.

Temporary SAS Data Sets are those which are allocated to the WORK library (often without the WORK designation specified, as this is the default).

The following two examples, which are identical in the way they operate, illustrate the creation of a temporary SAS Data Set:

```
data semicon;
set old.dataset;
run;

data work.semicon;
set old.dataset;
run;
```

One example of how this might save time is when you're doing two or more modifications in separate DATA steps, and you only need the final version to be written permanently. Here is a short example (with three DATA steps) of that scenario:

```
libname myperm '<--folder/subdirectory
specification-->';

data step1;

set myperm.dataset;

<--modifications-->;

data step1a;

set step1;
```

```
<--modifications-->;

data step2;

set step1a;

<--modifications-->;

data final;

set step2;

<--modifications-->;

run;
```

Question 120: Periods as Missing Values in Character Data

Why does a character string variable that has missing values indicated as '.' (Period) assign values to a new variable when the old variable equals '.' doesn't work?

Here's an example:

```
data temp; input a $;
if a='.' then b=9; else b=5;
cards;
4
.
5
6
3
.
;
proc print;
run;
```

This results in the variable B being all 5s.

A: The reason it doesn't work as shown above is that when SAS sees a '.' as a value for a character variable, it takes that to be a missing value, and since missing values in character variables are blanks (' '), SAS converts the period to a blank.

Replacing the '.' with ' ' in the IF statement will solve this problem.

```
data temp; input a $;
if a=' ' then b=9; else b=5;
cards;
4
.
5
6
3
.
;
proc print;
run;
```

Question 121: Transposing Row Data into Columns, and Columns into Rows

How can I transpose row data into columns and columns into rows?

A: Data can be re-arranged by programming in a DATA step, or by PROC TRANSPOSE. Both are explained briefly below.

************ PROC TRANSPOSE ****************************

PROC TRANSPOSE is documented in the SAS Procedures Guide.

/*** this program is a simple, straightforward
    transposition of the rows and columns of data ***/

```
data vert; input a b c;
cards;
5 5 5
5 5 5
7 7 7
7 7 7
9 9 9
9 9 9
;
proc print data=vert;
proc transpose data=vert out=horiz;
proc print data=horiz;

/***
PROC PRINT DATA=VERT;  results in this output

OBS    A     B     C

1      5     5     5
2      5     5     5
3      7     7     7
4      7     7     7
5      9     9     9
6      9     9     9
```

```
PROC PRINT DATA=HORIZ;   results in this output

OBS   _NAME_   COL1   COL2   COL3   COL4   COL5   COL6

1       A       5      5      7      7      9      9
2       B       5      5      7      7      9      9
3       C       5      5      7      7      9      9
***/
```

/*** This program creates customized variable names for the new (transposed) columns of data. These variable names retain some of the original (row) structure which consisted of pairs, hence the new variable names all begin either with 'A' or 'B'.

The ID statement in the PROC TRANSPOSE step assigns the new variable names from the previous VARNAME variable ***/

```
data temp; set vert; count+1; drop count varpre
varnum;

if count=3 then count=1; if count=1 then varnum+1;

if count=1 then varpre='A';

else if count=2 then varpre='B';

varname=trim(left(varpre))||trim(left(varnum));

proc transpose data=temp out=temp2; id varname;

proc print data=temp2;

run;

/***
the final PROC PRINT DATA=TEMP2;   results in the
following output

OBS   _NAME_   A1   B1   A2   B2   A3   B3

1       A       5    5    7    7    9    9
2       B       5    5    7    7    9    9
3       C       5    5    7    7    9    9
***/
```

```
/********** DATA STEP Program
***********************************
```
Some data structures may be reorganized more efficiently by
writing a DATA step program, which allows virtually any
customization necessary.

In the following example, each COUNTRY has four observations
contain in a REGION code and three years worth of data for each
REGION. The goal is to have all data for each country in a single
observation.

To do this, new variables must be created for each year within
each region, and values reassigned. The example is structured
with separate DATA steps for each operation to make the steps
easier to see, but most can be combined into one DATA step if
you prefer. (This also would be a good candidate for the use of
macros, but that's another topic.)
```
*******/
```

```
data in1; input country $ region $ y70 y71 y72;

cards;

Angola   N 2 4 8

Angola   S 4 8 2

Angola   E 6 5 9

Angola   W 4 7 .

Morocco  N 3 5 7

Morocco  S 2 7 4

Morocco  E . 6 2

Morocco  W 3 8 5

Zambia   N 6 2 4

Zambia   S . 5 3

Zambia   E 7 5 8

Zambia   W 5 8 2
```

;
/** DATA ONE sets up the new variables, named by combining
the REGION code with the name of each year variable, hence W
+ Y72 is WY72, the year 1972 data for the West region; as SAS
processes the observations, when each new country is
encountered, all the variables (including the temporary
 COUNTER) are set to missing or zero, and then, one by one, the
new variables are created (and RETAINED, or saved) until all
four REGIONS and all three years have been processed ***/

```
data one; set in1; retain ny70 ny71 ny72 sy70 sy71
sy72

ey70 ey71 ey72 wy70 wy71 wy72; drop region y70 y71
y72;

if country ne lag(country) then do; counter=0;

ny70=.; ny71=.; ny72=.; sy70=.; sy71=.; sy72=.;

ey70=.; ey71=.; ey72=.; wy70=.; wy71=.; wy72=.; end;

counter+1;

if counter=1 then do; ny70=y70; ny71=y71; ny72=y72;
end;

else if counter=2 then do; sy70=y70; sy71=y71;
sy72=y72; end;

else if counter=3 then do; ey70=y70; ey71=y71;
ey72=y72; end;

else if counter=4 then do; wy70=y70; wy71=y71;
wy72=y72; end;
```

/*** DATA TWO simply selects the last observation for each
COUNTRY, which now has all of its original data on a single 'line'
***/

```
proc print data=one;

data two; set one; drop counter; if counter=4;

proc print data=two;

run;
```

/*** THE RESULTS ***/
/*** PROC PRINT DATA=ONE; shows how the groups of variables are built, observation by observation ***/

OBS	COUNTRY	NY 70	NY 71	NY 72	SY 70	SY 71	SY 72	EY 70	EY 71	EY 72	WY 70	WY 71	WY 72	COUNTER
1	Angola	2	4	8	.	.	.	.	.	.	.	.	.	1
2	Angola	2	4	8	4	8	2	.	.	.	.	.	.	2
3	Angola	2	4	8	4	8	2	6	5	9	.	.	.	3
4	Angola	2	4	8	4	8	2	6	5	9	4	7	.	4
5	Morocco	3	5	7	.	.	.	.	.	.	.	.	.	1
6	Morocco	3	5	7	2	7	4	.	.	.	.	.	.	2
7	Morocco	3	5	7	2	7	4	.	6	2	.	.	.	3
8	Morocco	3	5	7	2	7	4	.	6	2	3	8	5	4
9	Zambia	6	2	4	.	.	.	.	.	.	.	.	.	1
10	Zambia	6	2	4	.	5	3	.	.	.	.	.	.	2
11	Zambia	6	2	4	.	5	3	7	5	8	.	.	.	3
12	Zambia	6	2	4	.	5	3	7	5	8	5	8	2	4

/*** PROC PRINT DATA=TWO; shows the final result of one observation for each country ***/

OBS	COUNTRY	NY 70	NY 71	NY 72	SY 70	SY 71	SY 72	EY 70	EY 71	EY 72	WY 70	WY 71	WY 72
1	Angola	2	4	8	4	8	2	6	5	9	4	7	.
2	Morocco	3	5	7	2	7	4	.	6	2	3	8	5
3	Zambia	6	2	4	.	5	3	7	5	8	5	8	2

Question 122: Collapsing Multiple Records

Is there any way to collapse multiple records?

A: In reading hierarchical data (like the PUMS Census files which have Household records followed by a varying number of Person records for each household) I'd like to extract certain person records and then create one record per household, with the person-record information retained in the final household record.

BASIC DATA: Hierarchical; primary data (e.g., Household) with multiple secondary entries (e.g., Person[s]).

OBJECTIVE: One observation per Household with original data preserved from multiple persons (in separate variables).

To do this operation, one must understand the structure of the target (final) data set records. They will have the original household information and for each person variable of interest (in our example these are personal income and race), there will be one variable (column) representing each person for each variable of interest.

So if you are extracting two people from each household (in our example these are Wife and Husband) and you are interested in two variables (income and race), you will end up with four variables in your final data set: Wife's income, Husband's income, Wife's race, and Husband's race.

EXAMPLE: Consider these data (original PUMS configuration of H and P record types, but *not* necessarily data that actually would be in the PUMS files -- this is a simplified, conceptual example):

rectype hhnum hhinc hharea inc sex race famstat H 413 8500 5 P 413 3500 M 1 H P 413 5000 F 2 W P 413 0 M 1 C H 414 5600 3 P 414 5600 F 3 S H 415 4650 8 P 415 4650 F 2 W P 415 0 M 2 H

Here we have hhinc (household income), hharea (location of household), inc (personal income), sex (gender of person), race (race of person), famstat (status in family: Wife, Husband, Child, Single).

When you run the PUMS program, you should get one observation for each P (person) record, and the household data (in my example HHNUM, HHAREA, HHINC) distributed across all the Person records for each household.
In case the data are not PUMS (and there is no canned program to rectangularize the data), this is how the above data would be processed into 'person' records (with household information retained):

SAS Example: data first; retain hhinc hharea; drop rectype; input @1 rectype $ @; if rectype='H' then input hhnum 3-5 hhinc 7-13 hharea 15; else if rectype='P' then do; input hhnum 3-5 inc 17-22 sex $ 24 race 26 famstat $ 28; output; end; cards; H 413 8500 5 P 413 3500 M 1 H P 413 5000 F 2 W P 413 0 M 1 C H 414 5600 3 P 414 5600 F 3 S H 415 4650 8 P 415 4650 F 2 W P 415 0 M 2 H ; SPSS

Example: input program. data list file='temp1.data' / rectype 1 (a). do if (rectype eq 'H'). + reread. + data list file='temp1.data' / hhnum 3-5 hhinc 7-13 hharea 15. + leave hhnum hhinc hharea. else if (rectype eq 'P'). + reread. + data list file='temp1.data' / hhnum 3-5 inc 17-22 sex 24 (a) race 26 famstat 28 (a). end case. end if. end input program. save outfile='whole.sav'.

The data then would look like: hhnum hhinc hharea inc sex race famstat 413 8500 5 3500 M 1 H 413 8500 5 5000 F 2 W 413 8500 5 0 M 1 C 414 5600 3 5600 F 3 S 415 4650 8 4650 F 2 W 415 4650 8 0 M 2 H and then you would be ready to make one line (observation) per household.

This could be done a number of ways, but perhaps the most 'obvious' (i.e., the one where it's most easy to see what's going on) is to make two data sets (one for W and one for H, rename all the variables that apply to the person (not the household), and then merge back together BY HHNUM, resulting in one line per household.

Here are programs that would do this for the example data above (assuming the data above are in an SAS data set called WHOLE with the variable names indicated).

SAS Example: data husb1 wife1; set whole; if famstat='H' then output husb1; else if famstat='W' then output wife1; data husband; set husb1; drop hhinc hharea famstat sex; rename inc=husbinc race=husbrace; data wife; set wife1; drop famstat sex; rename inc=wifeinc race=wiferace;

SPSS Example: get file='whole.sav' / rename inc=husbinc race=husbrace. select if (famstat='H'). save outfile='husband.sav' / drop hhinc hharea famstat sex. get file='whole.sav' / rename inc=wifeinc race=wiferace. select if (famstat='W'). save outfile='wife.sav' / drop famstat sex.

You have two data sets that look like this: HUSBAND: hhnum husbinc husbrace 413 3500 1 415 0 2 WIFE: hhnum hhinc hharea wifeinc wiferace 413 8500 5 5000 2 415 4650 8 4650 2

Note that the household variables (HHINC HHAREA) were dropped from the HUSBAND data base.
This is not necessary, as the same values are found in both H and W records; it's just cleaner and more efficient if they are merged in from one dataset only, rather than asking SAS to overlay them (so to speak).

Don't worry about this; just remember that in this situation, where the values for the household variables are the same across all members of the household (because of the way the PUMS data were read in the first place), it doesn't matter if they (HHINC and HHAREA) are in both HUSBAND and WIFE datasets, or just in one of them.

We also dropped the FAMSTAT and SEX variables, because these are useless in the final data set in this example. The new variables (HUSBxx and WIFExx) imply the sex and family status of the participants.

For example, if we created a HUSBSEX variable, all the values would be M, and for WIFESEX, all values would be F, so this would give us unnecessary information.

The final step is to merge these two 'halves' back together for your final analysis data set.

This is straightforward: SAS Example: data final; merge wife husband; by hhnum; SPSS Example: match files file='wife.sav' / file='husband.sav' / by hhnum.

And then, finally, your data will look like this: hhnum hhinc hharea wifeinc wiferace husbinc husbrace 413 8500 5 5000 2 3500 1 415 4650 8 4650 2 0 2

Question 123: Rectangular varying number of observations

My rectangular data file has varying number(s) of records for each person, and I'd like to collapse the data set so that there is one record for each person, but have the values for certain variables (such as COURSE attended, or STATE resided in) retained from all the original observations for that person.

How can I make one observation per Person with all values of one or more original variables preserved (in separate variables)?

A: You must know the maximum number of observations for any one person in your data. Once you know this, you can set up a program that copies values from the original (vertical) variable(s) into corresponding new (horizontal) variables, with the last observation for each person containing all values, then extract that last observation to create your final data set.

DATA: Here is a sample data array to be used in the examples below. It contains three persons and the cities they lived in during a particular time period. Assume the data are in a file called state.dat

PERSON	STATE	YEAR
1	Mississippi	1945
1	Alabama	1953
2	New Jersey	1937
3	New York	1949
3	New Jersey	1963
3	Hawaii	1979
3	Alaska	1985
4	Florida	1946
4	California	1955
4	Georgia	1996

Step 1: Read in the data and determine the maximum number of observations per person.

SAS Example:

```
data state1; infile 'state.dat' truncover;

input person 1 state $ 7-21 year 22-25;

proc sort data=state1 out=state2; by person;

data state3; set state2;

if person ne lag(person) then counter=0; counter+1;

proc freq data=state3; tables counter;

run;
```

```
SPSS Example:

data list file='state.dat' / person 1 state 7-21 (a)
year 22-25.

compute counter=1.

if (person eq lag(person)) counter=lag(counter)+1.

frequencies variables=counter.

execute.
```

The frequency table for the COUNTER variable shows the largest number counted for any one person. This is the number of variables you need to create to hold the largest number of different STATE values for any one person.

Step 2: Create the four new STATE variables (STATE1, STATE2, STATE3 and STATE4) that will hold the (potential) four names of the state(s) in which each person lived.

SAS Example:

```
data state4; set state3; length state1-state4 $ 20;

retain state1-state4;

if counter=1 then do; state1=state; state2=' ';
```

```
state3=' '; state4=' '; end;
else if counter=2 then state2=state;

else if counter=3 then state3=state;

else if counter=4 then state4=state;

run;
```

SPSS Example:

```
string state1 state2 state3 state4 (a20).

compute state1=state.

if (counter ge 2) state2=lag(state).

if (counter ge 3) state3=lag(state,2).

if (counter ge 4) state4=lag(state,3).

execute.
```

Step 3: Extract the observation with the most information about states lived in (which, by design, is the highest-numbered COUNTER value).

SAS Example:

```
/** In SAS we can use the LAST.PERSON technique to extract
the last (highest value of COUNTER) observation *************/

proc sort data=state4 out=state5; by person counter;

data state6; set state5; by person counter; if
last.person;

proc print; var person state1-state4;

run;
```

SPSS Example:

[x] In SPSS, we sort the data set descending, and then ask SPSS to extract any observation in which COUNTER is equal to or greater than the previous value of COUNTER.

```
compute sequence=$casenum.

sort cases by sequence (d).

compute compare=lag(counter).

execute.

select if (missing(compare) or counter ge compare).

list variables=person state1 to state4.

execute.
```

At last, you have one observation per person, with four variables containing the names of all states in which that person lived.

Question 124: Creating "Lag" variables

How do I create a lag variable?

A: This program creates a 'backward' lag variable (i.e., a variable that contains the previous value of VAR1) and a 'forward' lag variable (i.e., another variable that contains the next value of VAR1)

*******/ /*** the program
***/

```
data original; input var1; cards; 1 2 3 4 ; data one;
set original; backlag=lag(var1); sorter=_n_; proc
sort data=one out=two; by descending sorter; data
three; set two; forlag=lag(var1); proc sort
data=three out=final; by sorter; proc print; run;
```

/*** the output ***/
OBS VAR1 BACKLAG SORTER FORLAG 1 1 . 1 2 2 2 1 2 3 3 3 2 3
4 4 4 3 4 .

Question 125: Using Values Stored in an SAS Data Set as Macro Variables in a Macro

How can I run a number of successive macros each with different values for the macro variables without writing many different macro calls?

A: You may have a macro that runs PROC MEANS on a series of subgroups of your data, and each time the macro runs, it needs a different DATE and COMPANY number combination.

Let's say you have 10 different companies and 10 different dates for each company. You could set up a macro with two macro variables, as follows:

```
%macro mymac(date,company);

<macro specifications>

%mend mymac;
```

And then write 100 macro calls, like so:

```
%mymac(date1,company1)

%mymac(date2,company1)
.  .  .
%mymac(date10,company10)
```

Or you could store the date and company numbers in an SAS data set, and let SAS grab the values in 100 iterations of a macro %DO loop.

This program shows how to use data in an SAS data set to provide input to a macro through macro variables.
The problem is that we have companies who have been sued on particular dates and we want to get an average of their daily income for the period consisting of five days prior to the suit to three days after (9 days).

The example shows two companies, with data for one month
*****/

```
data one; input date : date9. company suittype income
@@;

format date date9.;
cards;
```

```
01FEB1992  1  .  144954   01FEB1992  2  .  598854

02FEB1992  1  .  224456   02FEB1992  2  .  337522

03FEB1992  1  .  254675   03FEB1992  2  .  643607

04FEB1992  1  .  194382   04FEB1992  2  .  551396

05FEB1992  1  .  374737   05FEB1992  2  .  434454
06FEB1992  1  .  264426   06FEB1992  2  8  763645

07FEB1992  1  .  254554   07FEB1992  2  .  672566

08FEB1992  1  .  244635   08FEB1992  2  .  588879

09FEB1992  1  .  154853   09FEB1992  2  .  775722

10FEB1992  1  .  234766   10FEB1992  2  .  456634

11FEB1992  1  .  544654   11FEB1992  2  3  553263

12FEB1992  1  .  484345   12FEB1992  2  .  684376

13FEB1992  1  7  174462   13FEB1992  2  .  737485

14FEB1992  1  .  294588   14FEB1992  2  .  958757

15FEB1992  1  .  354827   15FEB1992  2  .  845666

16FEB1992  1  .  264674   16FEB1992  2  .  267574

17FEB1992  1  .  154555   17FEB1992  2  .  676733

18FEB1992  1  .  244433   18FEB1992  2  .  753661

19FEB1992  1  .  334572   19FEB1992  2  6  684840

20FEB1992  1  .  233691   20FEB1992  2  .  475459
```

```
21FEB1992   1   .   154754   21FEB1992   2   .   569580

22FEB1992   1   .   274946   22FEB1992   2   .   337670

23FEB1992   1   4   264857   23FEB1992   2   .   238727

24FEB1992   1   .   233767   24FEB1992   2   .   866855

25FEB1992   1   .   134955   25FEB1992   2   .   944344

26FEB1992   1   .   184743   26FEB1992   2   1   692472

27FEB1992   1   .   154214   27FEB1992   2   .   238577

28FEB1992   1   .   137425   28FEB1992   2   .   844966

29FEB1992   1   .   134354   29FEB1992   2   .   546824

;
```

The next step is to sort the data set.

```
proc sort data=one out=two; by company date;
```

The next step is to make a separate SAS data set containing only the 'events', i.e., those dates on which a company was sued.

```
data events; set two; keep eventnum company date;

if suittype ne ' ' then do; eventnum+1; output; end;

proc print data=events;
```

Finally, the macro is used to run PROC MEANS for each of the six events, with means calculated on observations that occur between five days before and three days after each event. The entire macro runs six times (because there are six events). Each time the macro cycles, two macro variables are created from the corresponding values in the EVENTS data set:

XCOMP (the Company Number for each event) and XDATE:

(The date associated with the event). These values are plugged into the %DO loop as &XCOMP. And &XDATE. Notice that &XDATE.-5 represents five days before the event date, and &XDATE.+3 represents three days after the event date.

```
%macro events;

%do i=1 %to 6;

data _null_; set events;

if eventnum=&i. then do;

call symput('xcomp',put(company,8.));

call symput('xdate',put(date,8.)); end;

data temp; set two;

if company=&xcomp. and

date ge &xdate.-5 and date le &xdate.+3;

proc means data=temp; var income;

%end;

%mend events;

%events

run;
```

Question 126: Using an SAS Data Set as a 'Lookup' File for Merging

How to use an SAS Data Set as a look up file for merging?

A: This program creates an SAS data set in which each observation from part1 is matched with all four observations from part2 which have the same ORIGIN value.

This is not a merge, since some ORIGIN values groups (of 4) must be used over and over for the different observations (people) from part1.***/

```
dm 'clear log; clear output';

data part1;

* if _n_ gt 2 then stop;

input person origin pred;

cards;

1   1   1

2   1   2

3   1   2

4   2   1

;

data part2;

input origin distance;

cards;

1   1

1   3

1   4
```

```
1   5
2   3

2   1

2   3

2   4
3   2

3   3
3   1

3   5

4   4

4   6

4   5

4   1

;

proc sql;

create view both as

select a.origin,person,pred,distance

from part1 as a, part2 as b

where a.origin = b.origin

order by person;
```

In the CREATE statement just above, the new view BOTH is created; PART1 AS A, PART2 AS B assigns the codes A and B to the two input data sources; WHERE A.ORIGIN = B.ORIGIN says that the PROC is to match on the variable ORIGIN in both data sources; SELECT tells the PROC which variables to keep; ORDER is the final sort sequence; **/

```
data final; set both; /*<--this makes view into SAS
data set */
```

```
proc print;
run;
```

Question 127: Reading SAS Date values (and other numeric data) from a string variable

When you try something like 01-15-93 (January 15, 1993), SAS evaluates the numbers as if it were an arithmetic expression.

How does one give a date value (in readable format) to a new variable in an assignment statement?

A: First, create a new variable that reads '01-15-93' as an alphanumeric string, then use the INPUT function to read that string into a new variable.

EXAMPLE:

The first assignment statement creates temporary string variable X that contains the date string, and then the second assignment statement creates the 'real' variable date using the INPUT statement to input X with an INFORMAT of MMDDYY8.

The variable A is INPUT only to show how regular data can be INPUT in the same step with an assignment statement.

```
data temp; input a; drop x;

x='07-11-46';              /*<-- first assignment
statement   */

date=input(x,mmddyy8.);    /*<-- second assignment
statement */

cards;

5
4
6
7
5
;

proc print; format date date.;
run;
```

Question 128: Paired T-Tests- SAS Uses PROC MEANS (!)

What is a Paired T-Test?

A: A Paired T-Test is a comparison of means of two scores obtained from the same sample (i.e., the same subjects) or dependent (highly correlated) samples.

Null Hypothesis:
--no difference between means of the two scores
Example:
--group of students are given a pretest and a posttest
Basic Data:
--id number (optional), two continuous variables (integer or ratio measurement)
Assumptions and Requirements:
--two scores are drawn from normal populations with the same variance

Method:
--t-test
SAS has PROC TTEST for independent samples, but doesn't have a straightforward method for calculating a paired TTest.

It is done using a special option of PROC MEANS.

******************** SAMPLE PROGRAMS
****

SAS Sample:

*Note: The method of using PROC MEANS to perform a paired Ttest is documented in the SAS Procedures manual in the chapter on PROC TTEST, as one of the examples at the end of the section.

```
data one; input id pretest posttest;

diff=posttest-pretest;

cards;
```

```
1 54 86

2 64 75

3 75 84

4 64 53

5 36 75

6 46 85

7 35 64

;
 proc means mean stderr t prt;

var diff;

run;
```

The DIFF variable is the difference between each pair of scores (POSTTEST, PRETEST), and the T and PRT options give, respectively, the Student's t (for testing whether the population mean for DIFF is 0) and the probability of a greater absolute value for the Student's t value.

SPSS Sample:

```
data list free / id pretest posttest.

begin data.

1 54 86

2 64 75

3 75 84

4 64 53

5 36 75

6 46 85

7 35 64
```

```
end data.
t-test pairs=pretest posttest.
```

NOTE: probability levels are two-tailed. To obtain one-tailed probability, divide the two-tailed value by 2.

```
BMDP Sample (using program 3D):

/ input    variables are 3.

format is free.

/ variable names are id, pretest, posttest.

/ matched  variables are pretest, posttest.

/ end

1 54 86

2 64 75

3 75 84

4 64 53

5 36 75

6 46 85

7 35 64

/ end
```

Question 129: Computing points along the curve of a theoretical distribution

How can I compute points on the density, mass, or cumulative distribution function of a theoretical distribution (such as Normal or Gamma)?

A: The PDF, CDF, and SDF functions are available to calculate points on the probability density (or mass) function, cumulative distribution function, or survival function for many distributions.

The log of the density, CDF, or survival function can be computed using the LOGPDF, LOGCDF, or LOGSDF function.

Available distributions are the Bernoulli, Beta, Binomial, Cauchy, Chi-square, Exponential, F, Gamma, Geometric, Hypergeometric, Inverse Gaussian (Wald), Laplace, Logistic, Lognormal, Negative Binomial, Normal, Normal Mixture, Pareto, Poisson, T, Uniform, and Weibull.

Acknowledgment

http://en.wikipedia.org/wiki/SAS_System

http://www.usc.edu/its/doc/statistics/sas/faq/

Index

3-character extensions....115
32-bit operating system..195
Academic Computing Offer
....39
ACCDATA.......................147
Access Descriptor....143, 144
access rights.....................48
Accessing Auto call Macro
library..........................88
Accessing Sample Library
Programs......................90
active file.................190, 222
actual value.....................181
Adaptive Vector
Quantization.................99
Adding label to the new
point...........................212
ADXGEN macro definition
.................................88, 89
algorithms........................96
alphanumeric string......100,
254
alternative methods.........99
aludra.........110, 119, 131, 133
Analysis Survey Data Base
....98
arbitrary..134, 146, 182, 183,
207, 216
arbitrary example............146
arbitrary nickname. 207, 216
architectural changes.......58
Architectural Changes
Overview......................59
area value.......................208
ARRAY statements.........204
assignment statement.....86,
100, 106, 152, 181, 182,
254
automatic setup program. 47
Base SAS software61, 90, 91,
92
basic requirement...........109

Batch Processing.............218
batch Scheduler userid...203
behavior.................8, 44, 97
binary (encoded) data.....121
binary mode.....129, 157, 159
binary transfer........186, 198
binary transfer mode......198
BMDP.......................173, 257
braces............................204
built-in limitation...........151
BUNDLES folder..............34
BY statement....................77
BY variable.......................77
BY-value..........................73
bypass..............................19
Campaign Management..213
carriage control attributes76
carriage control characters
.................................75, 76
Carriage Return..............162
categorical predictors....103,
104
CEDA...............195, 196, 197
Changing name of a layer
.................................219
Changing the Internal Order
of Variables.................193
character variables....44, 78,
155, 232
character-based window 218
Character-to-Numeric
Conversions................106
Checking co linearity in
Logistic Regression......82
circumvent........................48
clicking path...................172
Client-Side Components
Volume 1......................32
co linearity diagnostics.....82
coding methods..............104
cold reboot power down...28

collapse multiple records 238
column number \.............124
columns into rows..........233
Comma-delimited data..178, 179, 182
command 'binary'....157, 159
command line......23, 50, 88, 89, 90, 91, 92, 117, 161, 163, 170
Command Prompt Window 120
command-line ftp....157, 159
comparison of means of two scores..........................255
complete......14, 26, 125, 166, 173, 217, 220
complex sampling designs 98
compressed data.............164
compressed local files.....165
COMSPEC parameter.......49
conditionally replace........68
constraints.......................170
converted directly...........202
Converting Access, Excel, and dBase-type files...139
Converting Old SAS FSEDIT Screens.....................161
Converting SAS Dataset...78
converts...........................232
copy and paste..................43
core..........10, 88, 90, 91, 92
correct terminal type......109
corresponding SCHEMA.116
COUNTER variable........243
covariates.........................171
cport 145, 159, 160, 185, 186, 196
create a lag variable........246
create an output data set..94
CREATE statement.........252
Creating a Variable indicating a Percentile. 72

Creating Aliases for Variable Names...........................21
Creating Design Matrix. .103
Creating Version 6.12 SAS Data Set......................216
Cross Environment Data Access.................195, 196
cross tabulation tables.....98
cumulative distribution function......................258
curly-brackets.................204
Current Output.................43
current Setinit information 36, 37
customization.............8, 235
cut and paste...............43, 54
Data Array.......................190
Data Flux Corporation Quality Knowledge Base 39
data matrices..................230
DATA Step.......................33
data storage.....................199
data-value lengths............56
database permissions.....203
Dataset.....21, 48, 64, 66, 78, 112, 121, 130, 167, 230, 240
date value........100, 147, 254
DATEPART function......148
DATETIME value............147
Dealing with Date Values147
decile ranks.....................72
decimal point...........108, 127
default engine.................201
default title.......................74
define a lattice...............208
delimited..140, 177, 178, 179, 180, 181, 182, 200, 214
delimiters.140, 177, 178, 179, 180, 181, 182, 183, 194
density....................205, 258
density function..............205
descriptive.................21, 98

design variables......103, 104
detection and removal
 software........................28
Determining Schema.......116
DIFF variable..................256
Disabling Macro Prompt..62
DISPLAY environment
 variable 109, 110, 118, 120
display graphical output. 118
DM statement..................211
DO loop...................227, 249
DOS file extension..........199
Double Space Output........56
double-spaced...................56
downloadable patch.........44
DROPs variables.............224
DSD option..............178, 179
dummy...................103, 104
Dynamic Data Exchange..64
empty squares.................162
entry point names.............58
equation..................108, 220
error related page faults. 215
Estimating the distribution
 of sample data............205
experimental option........167
Experimental Software.....93
export files......................214
Exporting SAS Dataset....112
F-tests..............................26
Failure to start-up..............23
FBA.................................76
final analysis data set......241
Finding your IP address..118
first directory..................199
first NOTE lines................85
Fixing Procedures............83
Floating Point Overflow
 Errors..........................171
FORMAT statement.......133,
 134, 135, 153, 154, 155
formatted differently........83
formatted values.....152, 153,
 155

Foundation..................59, 61
Functional-link nets.........99
future versions................216
Garbage Characters........126
Gauss..............................173
GIS action......................211
given word......................194
global statement..............94
GOPTIONS statement......86
header information..........45
hexadecimal...................177
Hiding code.....................71
hierarchical data.............238
Hierarchical Regression...25
highly correlated.............255
Host Internal Error 11......48
IF statement......33, 174, 175,
 232
imbedded decimal...........107
import....35, 44, 64, 66, 140,
 145, 161
Import Wizard...35, 44, 139,
 140, 141, 145, 200
Importing Data from Other
 Software......................151
incompatibility.......168, 206
independent.....7, 26, 59, 82,
 209, 255
indicator..........103, 104, 170
INFILE statement...177, 178,
 179
input data set.............72, 101
input data vector.............193
INPUT line......................227
INPUT sequences...........227
install SAS for Windows
 Version 9.x...................20
Installation of Software on
 Windows......................52
installation procedure......40
installation process..........36
Installing SAS 9.1..............19
Installing SAS for Windows
 ....20, 215

Installing SAS Windows 8.2 36
insufficient memory.........48
Intel-ABI platforms.........167
Interactive SAS................163
internal interface..............59
Invoke.......................212, 219
invoke SAS under UNIX.109
invoking SAS.....................85
invoking Version 7............23
ITS Public User Areas.....119
ITS Site Coordinator.........36
ITS User Rooms..............109
ITS-supported public user rooms...........................119
Kernel density estimation 205
kernel discriminant analysis 99
known bug.........................43
label parameters.............212
Launching SAS for UNIX 119
Launching SAS under UNIX 109
less-than-full-rank coding 104
LIBRARY libref...............134
LIBREF.....................87, 143
Line Feed........................162
linear models 14, 98, 99, 220
list of Metadata Server......61
load modules.....................58
log. 71, 81, 110, 119, 128, 133, 169, 196, 213, 251, 258
LOGISTIC MODEL statement......................82
Logistic Regression model 82
Lost Variables.................151
Low level...........................63
low-level OS interfaces.....59
lower-numbered releases 184
machine freezes................48

Macintosh SAS Program File...............................162
macro...8, 13, 60, 62, 63, 64, 71, 77, 78, 86, 87, 88, 89, 105, 247, 249, 250
macro %DO loop.............247
macro definitions.............88
Macro prompt...................62
macro variable value........86
macro variables 86, 247, 249
macro viruses...................63
main memory....................57
Making Windows stay in foreground.................211
mass.......................205, 258
maximum likelihood solution.......................171
medium security..............62
memory size invocation option...........................57
merge.......151, 174, 175, 239, 241, 251
metabrowse......................61
Micro-X or Mac-X..........118
microcomputer 110, 122, 218
minimum system requirements................19
Mips-ABI.........................167
mis-coded values.............152
mismatch..........................35
missing value. .180, 221, 232
missing values.154, 178, 179, 232
MOD...............................161
model selection methods..27
modified template............83
multi-co linearity.............82
multiple arguments........198
multiple iterations............48
multiple observations.....222
multiple platforms...........59
multiple presses.................54
multiple processors..........59
multiple RCMD options. 198

multiple secondary entries 238
multiple transport files....60
n equations......................101
n-way frequency...............98
Nadaraya-Watson kernel regression....................99
neural networks...............99
new platforms.................184
new spatial.....................208
NEWGROUP variable....108
NFS protocols..................166
nickname...87, 119, 120, 125, 186, 187
nobs...............................123
NOBYLINE system option 77
NOCLONE option.....41, 196
NODUPKEY option..........73
non convergent algorithms 99
non-existent directory......49
non-interactive mode.......74
nonparametric model...220, 221
nonparametric regression model...........................220
normal SAS data set name 169
NOSOURCE.....................81
Novell servers..................48
NT Service Pack 6............38
null hypothesis.................25
numeric data.....78, 100, 254
Numeric-to-Character Conversions...............106
OBS column.................45, 46
observation...12, 72, 73, 212, 222, 223, 224, 225, 227, 236, 237, 238, 239, 242, 244, 245, 251
observed sample data.....205
ODS Graphics...................30
ODS LISTING statement. 42

ODS OUTPUT statement 94, 97, 103
OLD............73, 124, 125, 144
old data............................186
old variable equals..........232
older versions of DOS......115
Older versions of SPSS...136
OLE...................................34
one-way............................98
opening page break..........68
Option FORMDLIM.........50
OPTIONS MPRINT...........21
OPTIONS statement.........45
ORIGIN value..................251
original configuration.......54
Original data structure...222
original data values.........152
original observations......242
original SCL code............161
original variable...............72
original variables....190, 191, 242
original variables preserved 242
outline.............................143
output. .8, 10, 27, 42, 43, 50, 56, 73, 74, 77, 94, 95, 96, 97, 103, 104, 105, 107, 124, 125, 126, 128, 129, 132, 143, 144, 148, 150, 154, 181, 182, 187, 233, 234, 239, 240, 246, 249, 251
Output Delivery System. .10, 17, 42, 83
Output Window.50, 126, 132
Outputting...............181, 182
overview document.........184
page break...................50, 51
Paired T-Test..................255
parameter estimates..26, 95, 220
Parametric density estimation..................205

parsing code....................170
particular statistic.............94
partition size...166, 168, 169, 170
partitioning......166, 167, 170
path expression...............185
PATH statement...............113
pc-to-host communication packages.....................186
Periods as Missing Values 232
permanent formats.........134
permanent SAS Data Sets 207, 230
person-record information 238
PIPE feature....................164
plus sign (+).......................61
pmenu.............................117
point layer...............210, 212
polygon selected point...208
Pop-up windows...............70
Portable file.............129, 133
post process.....................75
potential error inducing condition.....................48
predicted values......220, 221
predictor variables....99, 103
predictor vectors x2 and x3 25
predictors..........97, 104, 221
preliminary version..........93
Presence of Spyware while installing.....................28
Preserving Formatted Values.........................152
Probabilistic neural nets. .99
probability density.........258
probability-based random samples........................98
Proc Access.....................113
PROC ACCESS syntax....139
PROC COPY method......157, 189

PROC CPORT...60, 121, 122, 136, 145, 146, 157, 159, 160, 161, 195
PROC FREQ................22, 56
PROC LOGISTIC.......82, 83, 104, 171
PROC MIGRATE.....160, 195
Proc Mixed.......................57
PROC Mixed.....................57
PROC PHREG................204
PROC PRINT output........45
PROC PRINTTO..42, 50, 81, 128
PROC REG.....22, 25, 26, 82, 94, 95
procedural output.......75, 76
procedures....7, 8, 10, 12, 14, 48, 77, 83, 95, 98, 99, 105, 122, 145, 184, 220
PROGRAM action...........211
program statements128, 162
proper character.............162
PUT function...................152
Putting the value of BY Variable.........................77
random number generators 97
RANK procedure..............72
re-arranged by programming.............233
re-register..........................55
Reading HTML table........64
Reading in to SAS data files 177
Reading SAS Data Sets...199
Reading SAS Date values 100, 254
Reading the rest of Variables....................227
real ram..........................48
Rearranging Data...........222
recoded...........................192
Recoding Variables.........190

Rectangular varying number of observations 242
Redirecting SAS Log and Output..........................128
REG MODEL statement...82
Registered.........................55
regression model........26, 97
reinstate....................46, 117
Release 6.07...............76, 77
remote-logging................110
Removing duplicates........73
Removing Header Text.....45
Rename....................23, 219
rename the layer in batch 219
Renaming Entry Point......58
reorganized.....................235
Repetitive DATA steps...230
resole.............................230
RETAIN keyword...........225
return...50, 54, 86, 126, 145, 206, 215
root............................21, 188
Running DOS command. .49
Safe Mode.............29, 52, 53
Safe Mode Installation.....52
same designation..............35
Sample Code....................33
sample data array...........242
SAS across Different Systems......................184
SAS Add-ons...................172
SAS Catalogs...................161
SAS command line..........90
SAS Companion..............163
SAS Data Quality-Cleanse Software........................39
SAS Data Set......44, 55, 122, 124, 129, 130, 131, 134, 140, 141, 142, 143, 144, 145, 157, 159, 160, 185, 187, 189, 193, 230, 247, 251

SAS Data Sets....40, 115, 121, 139, 143, 158, 159, 160, 184, 185, 186, 187, 188, 189, 195, 199, 206, 207, 216, 230
SAS DDE program............62
SAS for Microcomputers.50, 183
SAS for Windows 8.2. 36, 38
SAS icon...........................48
SAS installation.........28, 70
SAS invocation................170
SAS Java Cmponents.......30
SAS Java Runtime Environment software. 30
SAS log...81, 83, 85, 93, 128, 145
SAS Macro Language Reference.....................71
SAS Shared Components CD.............................34
SAS Site Number.............85
SAS Syntax Editor Control 34
SAS System Viewer...32, 199
SAS ToolBox command line 117
SAS Transport Files136, 157, 184
SAS under UNIX Release 7 218
SAS User-Defined Formats 130
SAS/Access Interface......114
SAS/Access to Oracle......113
SAS/IML change..............97
SAS/INTRNET-Frequently asked questions............86
SAS/E9 for UNIX..............41
SAS/E9 for Windows.........41
SASUSER library..............23
SCAN function.................194
Scheduler...............203, 213
scheduler parameters.....213

scheduling engine executable file..............213
SCHOOL layer........208, 210
second directory..............199
Second- and higher-order neural nets....................99
Segmentation Violations. .57
SELECT Loop....................33
Selecting Observations in a Merge...........................174
Sending an SAS Dataset through e-mail............121
sending operating system 121
Sensitivity Analysis...........97
separately licensed product 39
series of subgroups.........247
set FTP download mode. 198
Setinit procedure.............215
Setting Program Editor Colors...........................117
Setting SAS System..........47
side-by-side delimiters. .178, 179
similarly-coded variables 190
simplified environment...52, 54
simultaneous equations. .101
simultaneous importation 189
single observation. .222, 235
site-license purchase......218
Size of an SAS Data Set...123
Software that works with SAS..............................173
Sound Designer.................55
special ANSI character...126
Special considerations in Release 7 and higher. .201
special delimiters.....177, 181
spline model....................220
split portions...................151

SPSS Value Label information..129, 131, 132
spss2sas program............132
Spyware or Adware intrusions.....................28
start up procedure............52
static...............................212
statistical procedures. .9, 96, 97
Statistical Technical Support........................96
stored compiled macro.....71
Storing Output Delivery System...........................42
Stray SAS processes..........28
string variable 100, 107, 108, 232, 254
subdirectory. .36, 37, 87, 111, 134, 145, 146, 188, 201, 202, 216, 230
Sun Workstation.....110, 218
supported..9, 19, 20, 41, 119, 198
suppress warnings............81
Suppressing Page Ejects...75
Suppressing the automatic printing....................74
survival function.............258
SYMBOLGEN....................21
symbolic names................21
system-configuration problem........................49
system's CD reader...........47
TAB separations..............181
telnet...............................218
temporary variable..........174
TEST statement.................25
text columns....................44
text format......................214
theoretical distribution. .258
threaded kernel...........58, 59
TITLE statement...............77
trailing number.............169
trailing zeroes.................106

translation.........41, 122, 186
transport files...60, 121, 137, 146, 157, 159, 184, 187
transpose row data into columns......................233
true SAS Date Set............157
true truncation................127
Truncation of SAS numeric values.........................127
turns off warnings.............81
tvl 123
typical scenario...............143
un-encoded file...............122
un-register.........................55
uncompressed data feed. 164
uncorrupted profile file...111
undocumented FILE........42
uninstall the SAS System. 70
unique id-number variable 151
UniTree...........164, 165, 184
UNIX uncompress command....................164
UNIX-based stat packages 173
unlabeled points..............212
unsafe...............................86
unsetting..........................110
usable.......................161, 201
USB Supplement.............215
USC distribution...............32
USC user rooms..............119
user feedback...................93
Using Compressed Data Stored on UNIX Disk. 164
Using Data Files Larger than 2 GB....................166
Using e-macs...................163
Using SAS Data (Transport File) in SPSS...............136
Using SAS for UNIX........118
Using SPSS Data.............129
Using Version 7..............206
uuencode process............122

uuencoded.........................121
v612 engine......................216
value labels..............133, 137
variable value...........86, 194
variant..............................199
VBA...........................62, 76
VECTOR command........190
verification.................19, 83
Version 6 \.......................207
Version 8. .17, 25, 27, 34, 86, 160, 161, 195, 216
Version 8.1........................34
Version 8.2....20, 35, 36, 38, 39
Version 8.x......................161
View Descriptor......143, 144, 145
virtual (swap file) memory 48
WC appendage................167
wildcard reference............60
Windows environment.....52
Windows ME platform.....20
Windows XP Home Edition 19
Windows XP Professional 19
WORK designation.........230
workbook..........................112
write out a TAB-delimited raw data file................181
Writing SAS Data Set into Raw Data.....................124
wsave...............................117
X command......................49
X Windows mode............110
X-Win..............................120
X-Win session..........119, 120
X-windowing environment 118
X-Windowing system.....218
xFS type file system........166
XPORT engine...60, 136, 217
-editcmd switch...............163
!sasroot..........88, 90, 91, 114

'backward' lag variable...246
'forward' lag variable......246
'housing' directory..........165
'Lookup' File for Merging
.....................................251

'real' variable date...........254
*.sd7 extensions in Version
9....................................115
#BYVAR...........................77
%LET statement................21

LaVergne, TN USA
22 September 2010
198129LV00008B/49/A